THE BEDFORD SERIES IN HISTORY AND CULTURE

U.S. Environmentalism
since 1945

A Brief History with Documents

Related Titles in
THE BEDFORD SERIES IN HISTORY AND CULTURE
Advisory Editors: Lynn Hunt, *University of California, Los Angeles*
David W. Blight, *Yale University*
Bonnie G. Smith, *Rutgers University*
Natalie Zemon Davis, *Princeton University*
Ernest R. May, *Harvard University*

THE BEDFORD SERIES IN HISTORY AND CULTURE

U.S. Environmentalism since 1945

A Brief History with Documents

Steven Stoll

Yale University

BEDFORD/ST. MARTIN'S   Boston ♦ New York

For our children, Batsheva, Katya, Elijah, Jaden

For Bedford/St. Martin's

Executive Editor for History: Mary V. Dougherty
Director of Development for History: Jane Knetzger
Developmental Editor: Sara Wise
Editorial Assistant: Laurel Damashek
Senior Production Supervisor: Joe Ford
Production Associate: Maureen O'Neill
Executive Marketing Manager: Jenna Bookin Barry
Project Management: Books By Design, Inc.
Text Design: Claire Seng-Niemoeller
Indexer: Books By Design, Inc.
Cover Design: Billy Boardman
Cover Art: Smokestacks Emitting White Smoke. Walter Geiersperger/Index Stock Imagery.
Composition: Stratford Publishing Services, Inc.
Printing and Binding: Haddon Craftsmen, an RR Donnelley & Sons Company

President: Joan E. Feinberg
Editorial Director: Denise B. Wydra
Director of Marketing: Karen Melton Soeltz
Director of Editing, Design, and Production: Marcia Cohen
Manager, Publishing Services: Emily Berleth

Library of Congress Control Number: 2006922726

Manufactured in the United States of America.

2   1   0   9   8   7
f   e   d   c   b   a

For information, write: Bedford/St. Martin's, 75 Arlington Street, Boston, MA 02116 (617-399-4000)

ISBN-10: 0-312-41076-X (paperback)
         1-4039-7152-8 (hardcover)
ISBN-13: 978-0-312-41076-6

Acknowledgments

Acknowledgments and copyrights are continued at the back of the book on pages 165–66, which constitute an extension of the copyright page.

Foreword

The Bedford Series in History and Culture is designed so that readers can study the past as historians do.

The historian's first task is finding the evidence. Documents, letters, memoirs, interviews, pictures, movies, novels, or poems can provide facts and clues. Then the historian questions and compares the sources. There is more to do than in a courtroom, for hearsay evidence is welcome, and the historian is usually looking for answers beyond act and motive. Different views of an event may be as important as a single verdict. How a story is told may yield as much information as what it says.

Along the way the historian seeks help from other historians and perhaps from specialists in other disciplines. Finally, it is time to write, to decide on an interpretation and how to arrange the evidence for readers.

Each book in this series contains an important historical document or group of documents, each document a witness from the past and open to interpretation in different ways. The documents are combined with some element of historical narrative—an introduction or a biographical essay, for example—that provides students with an analysis of the primary source material and important background information about the world in which it was produced.

Each book in the series focuses on a specific topic within a specific historical period. Each provides a basis for lively thought and discussion about several aspects of the topic and the historian's role. Each is short enough (and inexpensive enough) to be a reasonable one-week assignment in a college course. Whether as classroom or personal reading, each book in the series provides firsthand experience of the challenge—and fun—of discovering, recreating, and interpreting the past.

Lynn Hunt
David W. Blight
Bonnie G. Smith
Natalie Zemon Davis
Ernest R. May

Preface

By the end of World War II, Americans' relationship with nature had changed dramatically. New consumption patterns drove an industrial economy that exploited the earth in new ways, while the atomic age heightened Americans' awareness of the earth's fragility. During the postwar period, the environmental movement took shape throughout the country in innumerable local organizations as well as in national campaigns against pollution and economic development. Environmentalists reshaped the physical and ideological landscape of the United States, improved the health of its citizens, compelled the government to enact new legislation, and contributed to the major debates about natural resources, energy, the science of ecology, and the meaning of progress. This collection of primary sources illustrates the development and growth of the environmental movement in the United States since 1945 and illustrates its central voices, positions, and goals.

Part One, the introductory essay, presents a brief history of U.S. environmentalism and ties it to some of the pivotal events in U.S. history since 1945. The introduction begins with a discussion of the philosophical origins of the movement in nineteenth-century romanticism and explains how our modern conception of nature emerged in response to the revolutionary and industrial upheaval of the late eighteenth and nineteenth centuries. It traces the influence of romantic thought through the work of its most important American contributors—Thomas Cole, Henry David Thoreau, and John Muir. It also helps readers understand the historic dynamics of postwar America that expanded environmentalism's singular focus on protecting wild spaces into a broad, diverse movement that addressed issues such as growth, consumer habits, pollution, food safety, biological interdependence, climate change, and environmental justice, all of which relate fundamentally to consumption. The introduction emphasizes the impact of the protests of the 1960s on the environmental movement and the role of the federal government in enacting sweeping environmental legislation during the 1960s and 1970s. It also addresses the objections of anti-environmentalists, whose concerns about the economic impact of environmental policies have spawned powerful lobbies.

The thirty documents in Part Two are organized thematically to illustrate the issues outlined in the introduction. While they cannot possibly include every important strand of environmental thought or activism, they do demonstrate the breadth of the movement and reflect the thoughts and actions of people throughout American society—from the citizens of Santa Barbara coming to terms with an unprecedented oil spill to the citizens of the fictional nation of Ecotopia; from Mexican farmworkers resisting pesticide poisoning to a First Lady of the United States advocating beautification projects; from the neighborhood activists of polluted Love Canal, New York, to the members of the Intergovernmental Panel on Climate Change. Each document is introduced by a headnote that provides context and key information. To facilitate classroom discussion and inspire further study, this volume also includes five illustrations, a chronology of key events, a list of questions to consider, and a selected bibliography.

ACKNOWLEDGMENTS

I would like to thank several editors at Bedford/St. Martin's: Patricia Rossi, who first signed the book; her successor, Mary Dougherty; and Sara Wise, who demonstrated remarkable knowledge, ability, and patience in helping me finish it. Emily Berleth and Nancy Benjamin ably guided the manuscript through the production process. My academic reviewers offered exemplary advice and comment. They included Rebecca Conrad, Middle Tennessee State University; Mark Harvey, North Dakota State University; Douglas Sackman, University of Puget Sound; Kathryn Morse, Middlebury College; Ellen Stroud, Oberlin College; Matthew Klingle, Bowdoin College; and Bonnie Lynn-Sherow, Kansas State University. Adam Rome of Pennsylvania State University and Stephen Pitti and Barry Muchnick of Yale University suggested documents, as did Peter Harnick. David Blight, series editor and my colleague at Yale, read an early draft of the introduction and made many important suggestions.

Steven Stoll

Contents

Illustrations

PART ONE

Introduction: The Rise of U.S. Environmentalism

On July 16, 1945, a six-kilogram sphere of plutonium exploded over the New Mexico desert with a force equal to 20,000 tons of dynamite. It was not only the magnitude of the bomb that made it different from any other, but also its effects. Radioactive fallout traveled on the wind, thinning out over a large region during the following week. Twenty miles from the test site, it exposed a family to nearly lethal levels of radiation, and sensors detected it two hundred miles from the test site after four days. Then, on August 6 and 9, the United States dropped nuclear bombs on the Japanese cities of Hiroshima and Nagasaki, killing 105,000 people. In Hiroshima, 45,000 died almost instantly, and 20,000 others died during the following four months. Radioactive plumes shot high into the atmosphere, where they diffused in the high air currents, subjecting every rain forest, arctic tundra, Pacific atoll, arid basin, coastal forest, and alpine range; every city, suburb, and rural county; and every human on earth to low but continuing levels of radiation. Nuclear weapons released levels of radiation that had never existed on earth before, to which no organism or community had ever been exposed. The threat of fallout represented a new and disturbing kind of human unity, one in which the fate of all people became intertwined with the fate of the earth under the new regime of technological warfare.

1

During the half-century following these events, environmentalism emerged in the United States as both a philosophy and a political movement. Though it had many points of origin, diverse supporters and contributors, and no single goal, environmentalism, in almost all of its forms, expressed the belief that industrial production and its consequent patterns of consumption created ecological instability that brought into question the viability of modern societies. At different times and in a variety of ways, environmentalists demanded redress for the tendency of industrial economies to waste resources, chemically poison people and landscapes, consume space in the countryside, create garbage, and increase population. Environmentalists also sought to redefine human society itself as a subset of the global environment. Environmentalism cannot be understood without its nineteenth-century antecedents, but as a movement it did not appear until after 1945, when earlier concerns over pollution and wilderness merged with a rising global conception of an imperiled human future (page 3). By the 1970s, environmentalism consisted of many simultaneous concerns, which can be summarized as follows:

—A philosophy that identifies wild landscapes with wholeness and aesthetic beauty and asserts that such landscapes, along with their plant and animal species, possess an inherent value beyond any economic value.

—The legal protection of environments and species to prevent them from being absorbed into the industrial economy.

—The conviction that industrial societies, in their present form, are incompatible with natural systems and that human progress lies in the increasing knowledge and understanding of how best to live as members of plant and animal communities.

—A critique of excessive consumption, overpopulation, pollution, and destructive technology, such as nuclear weapons and chemical pesticides.

—The extension of human rights to include the right to clean and healthful homes and neighborhoods.

This book presents a wide range of documents that reflect the perspectives of the various people and organizations that shaped postwar environmentalism in the United States. The diverse documentary record of environmentalism reveals the movement's wide variety of political and social goals. In order to document the history of environmentalism, however, we must first define it, as well as the ideas that

The Earth from Space
This photograph, taken on December 7, 1972, by an astronaut on the *Apollo 17* mission to the moon, made the earth seem delicate and vulnerable. No other image became as important an icon for the environmental movement.
Courtesy of Earth Sciences and Image Analysis Laboratory, NASA Johnson Space Center <http://eol.jsc.nasa.gov>.

were central to its origins and development, such as romanticism, industrialism, and conservation.

The modern form of the word *environment* comes from an older word that we hardly use anymore: *environ*, to surround, to form a ring around, to encircle. Scholars have found the first recorded uses of the word at the very end of the fourteenth century, when a river would have been said to environ a forest or a hedge to environ a garden. Not until the 1830s did the English poet Thomas Carlyle use *environment* to mean a surrounding area or region. Beginning in the 1920s, *environmentalism* referred to the sum total of moral or social influences shaping a person or community. The meaning central to this book—a concern with the preservation of the environment and the politics or policies associated with that concern—did not appear in print until 1972. But there is something remarkable and significant about that first modern use of *environment* by Thomas Carlyle, when he wrote in his novel *Sartor Resartus* that "the whole habitation and environment looked ever trim and gay." It marked the first time that *environment* referred to a landscape from the point of view of an observer, someone looking out at it and thinking about it.

What happened in the years leading up to the 1830s to make people, especially in England, pay closer attention to the landscapes that environed them? The answer points us to one of the most important influences on the later development of the environmental movement, a view of nature that reaches back 150 years from 1945 to the beginnings of industrialism.

INDUSTRIALISM AND ITS DISCONTENTS

In building a context for environmentalism, one subject—industrialism—stands out from all others and forms the backdrop to almost every document in this volume. By the middle of the nineteenth century, a manufacturing economy, driven by mechanical advances, had taken shape in the United States. Industrialism is a way of organizing labor, capital, and environments toward the manufacture of goods. It is a particular way of making things, usually by assembling diverse raw materials with machinery in factories. Next to capitalism itself, no other transformation has had such remarkable environmental consequences because industrialism extracted plants, animals, fuels, and minerals in unprecedented quantities. Whereas individuals as part of households had made what they needed with their own hands for tens of thousands of years, they now mass-produced goods for others, *consumers* who began to purchase *products* with money.

Supporters of manufacturing claimed that it promised an unprecedented degree of comfort and security against want, but opponents argued that it promised only squalor, sickness, and hunger for workers. The persistent and passionate claims of opponents over the century from 1820 to 1920 resulted in child labor laws and safer working conditions. But in addition to the dangers it posed for workers, manufacturing also caused unheard-of environmental destruction. The consumption it encouraged created new sources of pollution spawning a generation of reformers in nineteenth-century New England who connected clean air and water to their social goals.[1] From that time forward, advocates of environmental regulation saw themselves as resisting or reforming industrialism in order to improve the lives of the people and places subjected to its effects.

By the end of World War II, industrialism had transformed the landscape in neighborhoods and rural districts across the country. Rather than take trains from city to city, people purchased automobiles with internal combustion engines that emitted carbon dioxide into the atmosphere and drove them on federal highways. The car culture changed the countryside, as people expected city services to follow them out along the interstates. Cars also made it possible for people to live farther away from where they worked. *Suburban sprawl* describes the creeping expansion of residential and commercial land uses into regions of low population density. Its identifying feature is the endless replication of the highway strip, consisting of fast-food franchises, gas stations, and shopping malls.

By the 1950s, the combination of ever-increasing air and water pollution with rapid changes in land use began to define new ways of thinking about industrial "progress" for many Americans. These citizens had all sorts of worries—that the motor car would blur the distinction between city and country beyond recognition (see Documents 6 and 25); that rural life would come to replicate all the material conditions of city life (see Document 27); that pollution would make living in cities unbearable, placing greater pressure on suburban and wilderness areas as people fled the smoggy cities; that consumption would absorb an ever-greater portion of the world's natural resources. Opposition to industrial production explains much of what has given twentieth-century environmentalism its force. Values such as biological diversity, natural beauty, and sustainability—which became central to environmentalism—came to represent an alternative vision of economics and the human good.

ROMANTICISM

Industrial production provoked an initial response—not in the 1950s, but in the 1850s—from a small group of intellectuals who articulated a counter-movement called romanticism that is crucial to understanding the origins of environmentalism. We can trace our modern conceptions of nature directly to the work of nineteenth-century painters and poets living in England and the United States.

Between 1750 and 1850, all over the English-speaking world, painters, poets, and essayists began to regard forests and mountains differently than they had before—not as empty, barren, and desolate places where they felt confused and afraid, but as places of contemplation and refuge from the stresses of rapid social and economic change. These intellectuals found plenty of reasons to look away from society. Bleak and sooty industrial towns like Manchester, England; the public Jacobin terror of Robespierre that marked the end of the French Revolution, and the following wars of Napoleon; and the passionless logic of scientific thinking and the questions it raised about the existence of God and the soul impelled writers and painters to turn to the sense of possibility that they discovered in landscapes untouched by the destruction and moral chaos of the modern world. In wilderness, they experienced "the sublime"—a feeling of awe and fear at the transcendent power of God. Human progress did not lie in supremacy over nature, but in submission to or concord with it. In this way, romantics articulated a contrary vision of human progress, one that gave no particular importance to economic growth and one that meditated darkly on the fate of modern societies.

No one exemplified the romantic sensibility with the same virtuosity as the artist Thomas Cole. Born in Lancashire, England, in 1801, Cole immigrated to the United States with his family when he was seventeen years old. He discovered the mountains of New York and painted them extensively over the next thirty years. *View of Schroon Mountain* (1838) is typical of his work (page 7). It depicts a quiet, almost mystical, moment from the point of view of someone alone in a forested wilderness, with the vast mountain as an object of reverence and reflection. In the twentieth century, advocates of rugged mountains and desert rivers used the same kind of images (see Document 1) to convince people who might never visit these places that they should care about them.

Among the American romantics, none is better known than Henry David Thoreau, born in Concord, Massachusetts, in 1817. The defining moment of Thoreau's career came when he spent twenty-six months living alone in a small cabin that he built on Walden Pond. There, Thoreau set down his simplified sense of material well-being against that of the majority of people in his society. Like Cole and Carlyle, Thoreau attracted attention because of the sharp distinctions he made between a simple life close to uncultivated landscapes and

Thomas Cole, View of Schroon Mountain, Essex, New York, after a Storm *(1838)*

Environmentalism owes its philosophical underpinnings to the romantic movement, here illustrated by the work of Thomas Cole. Romantics called scenes like this "sublime," referring to the feelings of fear and awe they felt in wilderness. Later romantics set out to preserve the places where they experienced these emotions. Oil on canvas, 99.8 × 160.6 cm. © The Cleveland Museum of Art, Hinman B. Hurlbut Collection, 1335.1917.

the furious movement of the economic world. Yet Thoreau did not champion wilderness in the same way that Cole did. Concord was a thoroughly cultivated countryside during Thoreau's lifetime, and he clearly felt more comfortable there than in the isolation of more distant forests. The journal he kept during a trip up Mount Katahdin in Maine, published after his death in 1862, reveals that Thoreau was truly anxious—even terrified—at the rocky cloudscape he discovered at the precipice. Yet other romantics seemed to be moving in another direction, toward a sense of belonging to wilderness, not fearing it.

The writer John Muir, who followed Thoreau later in the century, had none of the same misgivings about wilderness. Muir emigrated from Scotland to Wisconsin as a child. As a young man, he sailed around Cape Horn to San Francisco, California, after an accident he suffered while working in a factory left him blind in one eye. In the summer of 1869, he entered the Yosemite Valley, in the Sierra Nevada, and wrote about the experience in a journal later published in 1911 as *My First Summer in the Sierra*:

> No pain here, no dull empty hours, no fear of the past, no fear of the future. These blessed mountains are so compactly filled with God's beauty, no petty personal hope or experience has room to be. Drinking this champagne water is pure pleasure, so is breathing the living air, and every movement of limbs is pleasure, while the whole body seems to feel beauty when exposed to it as it feels the camp-fire or sunshine, entering not by the eyes alone, but equally through all one's flesh like radiant heat, making a passionate ecstatic pleasure glow not explainable.[2]

Muir's embrace of wild places as warm and welcoming opened a door for later environmentalists. He founded the Sierra Club in 1892 to lead city people into the mountains, where he hoped that they would learn to see granite peaks and glacial valleys as he did. The Sierra Club also suggested the possibility of collective action to protect the places that Muir loved. Like earlier romantics, such as the English poet William Wordsworth, who moved to keep railroads out of the Lake District in England, Muir believed that the retreats where he and others felt such strong emotion were worth defending against the forces of technology and economic development.

During the first decade of the twentieth century, Muir and the Sierra Club attempted to prevent the city of San Francisco from building a dam across the Hetch Hetchy Valley inside Yosemite National

Park. Muir called the business and civic leaders who advocated for this project "temple destroyers, devotees of ravaging commercialism." "Dam Hetch Hetchy!" he thundered, "as well dam for water-tanks the people's cathedrals and churches, for no holier temple has ever been consecrated by the heart of man."[3] San Francisco won its case when Congress voted in 1913 to build the dam and dedicate the valley as a reservoir. With the building of that dam, the first twentieth-century attempt to place romantic values over the forces of economic growth failed.

CONSERVATION VS. ENVIRONMENTALISM

The Hetch Hetchy controversy provoked principled disagreement among supporters of wilderness with the way that government experts and progressive-era politicians conceived of progress. Conservationists who valued economic development above mountain retreats offer a contrast against which we can understand how environmentalism took shape and what made it distinct. Conservation placed values on natural resources for their economic potential, and it began out of concern for resource scarcity, if not ecological fragility. The principles of conservation were first proposed by the nineteenth-century scholar and congressman George Perkins Marsh, whose book *Man and Nature* (1864) argued that humans had changed the world on a geological scale. Marsh documented the ways that civilizations had turned humid regions into arid deserts by removing tree cover and how they had caused erosion, sending silt down mountainsides to build up in rivers and harbors. Since people could change the earth, said Marsh, they had a moral responsibility to manage it.

Conservationists believed in the most efficient possible use of landscapes to regulate what they defined as the natural wealth of the United States—its forests, farmland, minerals, and game animal populations. It was conservationists in government, including President Theodore Roosevelt and Chief Forester Gifford Pinchot, who supported the city of San Francisco and its plan to dam the Hetch Hetchy Valley. Dams not only kept water from running to the ocean, conserving it for the use of people, but the force of the water impounded behind them could be used to generate electricity. Dams prevented waste and created energy—two very attractive outcomes for conservationists. Conservation aimed to maintain an abundance of exploitable resources in order to ensure economic growth.

The tension between Muir's romanticism and conservation faded with Muir's death in 1914. World War I, the Farm Crisis of the 1920s, the Great Depression, and the entry of the United States into World War II in 1941 overshadowed debate about the uses of wilderness. In the meantime, President Franklin Roosevelt's New Deal government embarked upon some of the most astonishing hydroelectric projects in human history, including the Tennessee Valley Authority—a network of thirty-four dams meant to modernize life and economy in a 41,000-square-mile region. Emerging from the war years with a sense of triumph and an unflinching mission, the Bureau of Reclamation (the federal agency that manages water resources) declared in 1946 its intention to conserve the flow of the Colorado River drainage to drive the agricultural and urban development of the Far West.

Just as the Bureau of Reclamation geared up for an era of massive water-storage projects, a group of hikers and wilderness enthusiasts began to take notice of its activities. A variety of intellectuals interested in land and its preservation came of age after the 1930s. They included David Brower (Document 5), Ansel Adams (Document 1), Aldo Leopold (Document 11), Robert Marshall, Marjory Stoneman Douglas (Document 2), and others who rejected the utilitarian conception that the best use of any landscape is to provide raw material for capitalist enterprise or national wealth. Instead, they argued for the scenic value of landscapes and for preserving them along with their plant and animal communities. Movements are often born of specific moments when their adherents' goals and principles come into sharp relief against prevailing views. That is what began to happen in the 1950s, when some of these wilderness advocates confronted the conservationist agencies of the United States.

No controversy contributed more to the formation of a distinct environmental ethic than the question of whether to flood Dinosaur National Monument, a unit of the national park system straddling the border between Utah and Colorado, to build a hydroelectric dam. In 1954, the Bureau of Reclamation made public a plan to control the entire Colorado River drainage with dams at a number of key points, including one that would flood Dinosaur National Monument.[4]

No one had ever stopped a reclamation project, and almost no one had ever wanted to stop one. Conservationists won over the public with the promise that if Americans entrusted their government with the nation's natural resources, the government would provide future generations with the same or greater affluence as that enjoyed by the present generation. But the leadership of the Sierra Club insisted that increasing wealth did not always represent progress, and that progress should also be measured by the capacity of a society to restrain its growth. This idea of restraint, combining concerns about overconsumption and the long-term survival of places of natural beauty, began to define a distinct movement. The battle over Dinosaur transformed the Sierra Club into an organization capable of national political action in defense of wilderness. The ensuing negotiations, public attacks on government data, and rising popular support convinced the Bureau of Reclamation to abandon the dam and Congress to insert a clause into its appropriations bill exempting national parks from future reclamation projects.

In saving one canyon, however, the lovers of wilderness gave away another. In 1964, Glen Canyon, also part of the Colorado River drainage (though not part of the national park system), disappeared under Lake Powell to become one of the largest and most important water-storage basins in the West. Some among the Sierra Club's political allies accepted this as a necessary political evil, but Sierra Club director David Brower lamented the bargain that resulted in the Glen Canyon Dam, which was 1,560 feet long and 25 feet thick, and rose almost 600 feet above the Colorado River (see Document 5). The Sierra Club challenged an American article of faith when it attempted to turn Congress against a dam: the faith that human progress and economic progress are the same.

CRITICIZING CONSUMPTION

Environmentalism did not have a single point of origin. Wilderness preservation was the most visible example of an alternative vision of progress, but there were others. In the 1960s, protest over American involvement in the Vietnam War quickly absorbed other issues, becoming a critique of American life and politics, including attitudes toward and uses of the environment. Student movements formed to protest abuses of the environment in the same way that they had formed to resist the war. Politicians, including Presidents John F. Kennedy and Lyndon Johnson, made statements against air and water pollution, as did the League of Women Voters and other women's organizations throughout the decade. Lady Bird Johnson's efforts to pass the Beautification Act of 1965 (Document 24) came out of the same desire to clean up the environment for the next generation. More generally, many people now believed that industrial society consumed prodigiously, expanded recklessly, and alienated people from nature. With nuclear war a very real possibility in the era of the Cuban Missile Crisis, it seemed that technological civilization would annihilate itself. From within this climate, a vast array of interests coalesced as a movement that formed a subset within the counterculture of the 1960s.[5] Throughout the 1960s and 1970s, the environment took on political resonance in Congress, which responded to electoral pressure and evidence of chronic pollution by passing the most ambitious environmental legislation ever enacted. Many of the arguments of that time swirled around the question of consumption and growth.

At its core, environmentalism is a critique of consumption. Americans' demands for an increased standard of living seemed limitless in the 1950s. But at the very moment that politicians celebrated the postwar affluent society, a new generation of thinkers began to reevaluate the capacity of the earth to sustain a global rise in consumption.

The growth of industrial society depends on the extraction of raw materials from forests, farmland, oceans, and mineral-rich valleys, transforming these landscapes to reflect the interests of capitalists often without regard for the continued existence of plant and animal communities. Environmental economists such as Herman Daly argued that economic growth followed a pattern not found in the rest of nature. Natural environments change, but they do not endlessly expand. They do not feed off distant supplies of nutrients and energy, but use only what is immediately available, and their products are easily broken down into basic elements for use again, the way a fallen forest tree quickly becomes home for funguses, before returning to soil. Environmentalists pointed out that economic systems shared none of these qualities, that they posited *infinite* expansion with models and forecasts that paid no attention to the capacity of environments to support them. Anxiety about growth also extended to a much older fear—that there were too many people on earth.[6]

In the midst of unprecedented postwar economic expansion, few Americans noticed or worried that humanity was rapidly increasing in number. It took most of human history, or about two million years, for the earth's population to reach one billion people, a mark it reached around 1800. It took only 130 years to add the second billion. The third billion came thirty years later, and the population reached four billion in just the fourteen years between 1960 and 1974. Growth advocates saw only progress in these numbers, but a minority of intellectuals and political economists saw something else—proof that humans would eventually consume themselves out of existence. Both sides looked back to the writings of Thomas Robert Malthus, an English parson who lived during the eighteenth century and whose *Essay on the Principle of Population* (1798) argued that the human population would always outpace the food supply, providing a natural limit to material progress.[7] Malthus said that while humans reproduced geometrically (by factors: 2, 4, 8, 16), food increased arithmetically (by successive units: 1, 2, 3, 4). It might not seem like a very striking or surprising observation — Malthus himself saw it as obvious — but it utterly shocked intellectuals of Malthus's time and after. Malthus's essay implied that the projected affluence of any society was pinned to agricultural production and thus had fixed natural limits.

DECLARATIONS OF INTERDEPENDENCE

Malthus's theory, however, was based on surprisingly little evidence for how environments actually functioned. (Malthus himself knew almost nothing about agriculture and seems to have never understood the stunning rise in productivity that had taken place over the previous two hundred years, eliminating famine in England by 1624.) In order to understand how or whether economic growth strained the earth's systems or its agricultural capacity, environmentalists of the 1960s needed actual data, which they found in the emerging science of ecology.

Ecology is the science of biological interdependence. The idea that living things, along with their natural environments, change and create each other originated in the work of Ernst Haeckel, a German zoologist and advocate of Darwin's theory of evolution, who coined the term *ecology* in 1879 to describe "the many and various relations of plants and animals to each other and to their environment."[8] *Ecology* is Greek for *house* or *dwelling*, suggesting that people could study these natural communities as microeconomies. Just as money and food flow through human households, so solar energy and nutrients flow through plant and animal communities. In time, ecologists came to understand these communities as dynamic, living entities existing on many levels, in parallel versions, from cell to organism to region to planet to universe. This interconnectedness is best expressed by *ecosystem*, a term first proposed by the British ecologist Arthur B. Tansley in 1935. The ecosystem concept lies at the foundation of the science of ecology, providing a testable unit for environmental stressors (pollution, development) and the effects of change on species and populations.

Ecology is not the same as environmentalism, but the two are related. Many ecologists proceed along some of the same assumptions that environmentalists use. Ecologists tend to believe that humans cause the decline of landscapes and that wilderness represents pure forms of nature (though many ecologists have recently begun to think about humans as part of natural landscapes and not simply as forces of disturbance; environmentalists have done the same).[9] Most important, ecological science has provided the environmental movement—long dependent on aesthetic judgments of beauty and scenic value—with hard data about the consequences of economic development in actual landscapes. For example, ecology forms the basis of the environmental impact reports stipulated by the Environmental Protection Agency (EPA) to be completed before anything can be built in sensitive areas, such as shorelines. It is also the foundation of the Endangered Species Act of 1973, which provides legal protection to animals if their populations fall below certain thresholds. But the field of ecology has contributed more to the environmental movement than data. Whereas industrialism obscures our dependence on the ecosystems that sustain us (by providing us with packaged meat and canned peaches), ecology has made those systems visible.

In its most general form, ecology can be boiled down to four maxims, best expressed by biologist and activist Barry Commoner (Document 13):

1. *Everything is connected to everything else.* This is the central insight of ecology—that the universe is a series of interrelated parts on many different levels, with nothing outside of the system.

2. *Everything must go somewhere.* Waste is an illusion, since what people discard ends up in other organisms—the way that pesticides are found concentrated in fish, for example.

3. *Nature knows best.* As Commoner explains, "any major man-made change in a natural system is likely to be *detrimental* to that system."

4. *There is no such thing as a free lunch.* In other words, any gain will come with consequences. Sharp rises in the gross national product will be accompanied by sharp rises in solid

waste and pollution from manufacturing. Human actions in the environment linger, even those actions we judge positively in other ways.

Though ecologists find much to debate about these premises (especially the extent to which humans damage the landscapes they change), most all accept them, whether they study humans in cities or ants in tropical rain forests. Commoner's four premises describe not only a systems approach to nature, but an ecological society.

An ecological conception of human society emerged from the Great Depression, finding expression in the works of Lewis Mumford, who cofounded the Regional Planning Association of America in 1923 and later wrote *The City in History* (1961). Mumford supported limited-scale planning, emphasizing pedestrians and not automobiles, and sought to integrate city and countryside. *The Land*, a journal published briefly in the 1940s, became a focal point for conservationists looking for a more expansive vision of nature and society in the years following the drought and dust storms on the Great Plains. On the same subject, biologist Paul Sears published *Deserts on the March* in 1935, in which he experimented with the notion that societies risked collapse when they exceeded ecological limits.

The greatest example of this early generation of environmentalists was Aldo Leopold, whose work became part of the intellectual foundation of environmentalism. After graduating from the Yale School of Forestry in 1909, Leopold joined the United States Forest Service and operated a predator control program in the desert Southwest. Although he encouraged the killing of wolves, mountain lions, and coyotes in the interest of hunters and cattle ranchers, Leopold eventually concluded that such efforts badly damaged the larger environments of which predators formed a crucial part. In "Land Ethic," Leopold argued for the existence of "biotic communities" that include humans (Document 11). Leopold not only helped to define wildlife ecology, but he identified humans as members, thus making them morally responsible for the viability and continuance of wilderness environments.

Yet the early ecological thinkers tended not to think about the day-to-day ways in which people affected environments by what they consumed. Consumption changed in the twentieth century. Humans became part of pollution streams—the byproducts of their consumption consisted of substances that could not be absorbed into ecosystems (for example, plastics and automobile exhaust). A forest recycles its plants and animals, breaking them down into the elements basic to all life. Industrial pollution does not break down easily (or at all) and has other chemical qualities that poison soils and organisms. Some substances such as carbon dioxide, although common on earth, had never before been released into the atmosphere in such large quantities. In other words, industrial society changed the consequences of human consumption.

By the 1960s, environmental concerns seemed urgent because millions of Americans had started to consume in radically new ways, none more radical than the use of synthetic chemicals. A panorama of chemicals in the forms of plastics and pesticides—compounds that had never existed on earth before—came onto the market, including dichloro-diphenyl-trichloroethane, or DDT. First synthesized in 1874, DDT had no known use until 1939 when Paul Hermann Müller discovered its insecticidal properties. It had no apparent toxicity to humans. What few people knew until the 1960s was that animals stored DDT in their fatty tissues, with many implications for human health and the environment. This is where ecology and environmentalism united, in a book by a marine biologist who helped to shape a popular movement founded on the interconnectedness of all living things.

The author was Rachel Carson and the book was *Silent Spring*, published in 1962. Conservationists had written about depleted resources and squandered wealth for a century in works such as Fairfield Osborn's *Our Plundered Planet* (1948) and William Vought's *The Road to Survival* (1948). But *Silent Spring* did something entirely different. It told readers that their own choices and decisions mattered in the larger world; that chemicals like DDT did not discriminate, but were, in fact, *biocides* with the potential to destroy all forms of life; and that the companies that manufactured DDT cared nothing about the health of the people who used it. Most of all, Carson wrote not about endangered Sierra valleys or the Grand Canyon, but about the common landscapes of America, insisting that the danger existed not in remote places, but in our gardens, lawns, and neighborhoods. Carson used ecology to show Americans the consequences of their consumption by explaining just what happened to pesticides once they left spray nozzles—how they dripped from leaves into soils, entered water tables and streams, and ended up in the bodies of fish that were then eaten by other animals and people. Carson stunned the nation with the simple revelation that consumption in industrial society could erode the very fabric of life.

Industrialism extended the boundaries of human impact on the environment. Until the twentieth century, the changes people made to environments affected them only locally. People have been known to destroy their ability to live in certain places, forcing them to migrate for fertile soils or animals to hunt, but they usually found it possible to escape into new territories of relative abundance. With new industrial capacities, factories polluted rivers far downstream, and hunters seeking bison tongues and whale blubber traveled by railroad and steamship to places once far distant from city markets. No one in the nineteenth century knew or imagined that the smoke rising from coal-burning cities would change the earth's atmosphere. By the time millions of people began to drive around in millions of automobiles, each its own carbon dioxide–producing machine, the human effect on environments, including the earth's climate, had become global.

The earth's atmosphere works like a greenhouse: It traps solar radiation, making life on earth possible. *Climate change* describes a rise in the earth's temperature caused by an increase in the concentration of certain gasses, especially carbon dioxide. That these gasses enhance the capacity of the atmosphere to trap solar heat can be demonstrated experimentally and is not questioned by scientists. Furthermore, ecologists and geologists do not question whether the earth is warming. According to the EPA, since the 1750s atmospheric carbon dioxide has increased 30 percent, leading to an increase in the earth's temperature of one degree Fahrenheit over the last century.[10] The ten warmest years since 1860 (when record keeping began) have all occurred since 1990, with 1998 the warmest, 2001 the second warmest, and 2003 the third warmest years. A seasonal lake now forms at the North Pole, and the melting ice caps now cause a yearly rise in ocean levels of 0.1 inches.

Whether humans have been the cause of global warming became the subject of vigorous debate in the 1980s and 1990s, when strong scientific data did not yet exist. The debate quickly absorbed policymakers and politicians, many of whom argued that no scientific basis existed for the claims that the earth would continue to warm. The issue seized public attention briefly in the summer of 1988, when NASA scientist James Hanson testified before Congress that the earth was warming. Politicians and business leaders assailed Hanson, and even some scientists believed that he had gone beyond the available data when he made this statement. The same year, in response to this confusion, the World Meteorological Organization and the United Nations Environmental Programme established the Intergovernmental Panel on Climate Change (IPCC) to assess all the scientific data available and the extent and risks of human-induced climate change (Document 16).

The IPCC prepared a pivotal report in time for the United Nations Framework Convention on Climate Change, which convened in Kyoto, Japan, in 1997. The Kyoto Protocol, which emerged from that convention, proposed world cooperation in reducing the production of carbon dioxide. Although it seems like an issue that should have unified environmentalists and strengthened their arguments against destructive technology and overconsumption, political forces within environmentalism eroded any sense of unity.

WHAT IT MEANS TO BE GREEN

Environmentalism proposed an alternative vision of progress, and by the 1970s, environmentalists employed politics to achieve their goals. Some wondered when environmentalism would develop into a political issue with the same resonance as the Cold War and become a force that might underlie a national campaign for the presidency. During the same time, the Vietnam War provoked unprecedented protests among college students, who invented a variety of tactics intended to turn public opinion against the war. One tactic was the teach-in, in which students occupied campus buildings where they made speeches, held discussions, and performed music and dramas. When Senator Gaylord Nelson of Wisconsin gave a speech in 1969 in which he called for a national teach-in on the environment, the response overwhelmed him. Students from across the country went to work on the project, and they set a date, April 22, 1970. Earth Day turned into the largest and cleanest demonstration in American history (Document 19). Twenty million people assembled in hundreds of communities across the country to throw giant earth balls, hear speeches from mayors and ministers, and sing. Kindergarten and elementary school children learned about ecology throughout the day and then marched outside to plant trees. State legislatures passed bottle bills to encourage recycling. For the first time, environmentalism looked like a mass movement, like it expressed a belief in health and beauty that most Americans shared.

Environmentalists assumed that government would serve as the mechanism for positive change, and they took it as their task to move the federal government to pass laws that would create standards for clean air and water, laws protecting the rights of people to live without fear of pollution, as when Congress banned the use of DDT in 1972. People throughout American history have believed that they could prevail upon legislators to shape law and policy. Environmentalists followed abolitionists, populist farmers, women demanding the right to vote, and civil rights leaders in this same desire for reform. Even as environmentalists argued against economic growth as a model of progress, they represented an older and deeper desire for moral progress. Since the Great Depression, Americans had come to expect government to expand its regulatory power as social needs demanded. Congress and President Richard Nixon responded with a remarkable series of acts, including the revised Clean Air Act of 1970; the sweeping National Environmental Policy Act of 1970, which created the Environmental Protection Agency and the Council on Environmental Quality and required environmental impact statements for all construction projects affecting land owned by the federal government; the Federal Water Pollution Control Act of 1972; and the Endangered Species Act of 1973.

The communities that participated in Earth Day wanted clean air and water and a government that would continue to respond to these problems. They did not favor or call for profound changes in the ways that Americans lived. Others, however, did just that. The organizers of Earth Day included students who had learned protest from the antiwar movement. They saw the war and the decline of the natural environment as linked to the same political and economic systems, both in need of radical reform. Countercultural protest regarding war, race, and equality found an environmental analogue in the use of *green* as an adjective and noun. This usage dates from 1971 (in the form of Greenpeace, an American organization) and 1974 (in the form of the German Green Party). The green movement is generally defined by the desire for pure foods (as opposed to those produced by industrial agriculture), for pedestrian spaces (as opposed to highways and cities built around automobiles), for renewable sources of energy (as opposed to petroleum and nuclear power, both of which depend on large, centralized industrial systems), and for a decentralized society in general that would result in a larger sphere for personal expression. While the dominant culture fell in love with space exploration, interstate highways, and skyscrapers, green culture embraced a book by E. F. Schumacher, a German-born British economist, titled *Small Is Beautiful* (1973), which argued that economic growth was out of control and the affluent countries wasted natural resources.[11]

Environmentalism gained an unlikely spokesman in Theodor Seuss Geisel, an author of children's books known as Dr. Seuss. In *The Lorax* (1971), a faceless industrialist called the Once-ler discovers the land of the Truffula trees and invents a product that "everybody needs." Just as he cuts the first tree, a little man appears: "'Mister!' he said with a sawdusty sneeze, 'I am the Lorax. I speak for the trees.'" The Lorax calls the Once-ler "crazy with greed" for doing nothing more extraordinary than establishing a factory and pursuing a program of "biggering." But the Once-ler pollutes the air and water as he clear-cuts the forest. All the wildlife is forced to migrate. When the Once-ler finally cuts the last Truffula tree, he destroys the basis of the industry, leaving the region denuded and vacant. *The Lorax* asks readers to identify with the odd creature who speaks for the trees, not with the personification of economic growth, depicted as immoral and self-defeating. Never before had environmentalism found so popular a voice or spoken with so much influence.

The book even inspired an anti-Lorax story, published by the National Wood Flooring Association: *The Truax* (1995), written by Terri Birkett, in which a kindly logger (Truax) explains conservation forestry and the benefits of forest products to a daffy tree defender (the Guardbark). This book provides a window into the opposition to environmentalism that arose in the 1980s, after the election of President Ronald Reagan. Political conservatives believed that humans should exercise their hand in the world without hesitation and that consumption created wealth: They never accepted green assumptions. Conservatives railed against environmentalism, calling it economically destructive and even religiously threatening for the way it appeared to locate spiritual authority in nature. The most visible representative of what came to be known as the "wise use" movement was James G. Watt, secretary of the interior during Reagan's first administration. In the 1970s, an organized resistance to the federal ownership of public lands—the Sagebrush Rebellion—took hold in eleven western states. Nevada, along with four other states, passed bills in 1979 authorizing the seizure of land under the control of the Bureau of Land Management to make it available for private and public uses. Watt and Reagan declared themselves "sagebrush rebels," with Reagan sending thanks and greetings to a Sagebrush convention in Salt Lake City and promising that his administration would work to return control of natural resources to the states. The movement faded from public attention and from the agenda of the White House when Watt resigned in 1983, but the real cause of its demise was the failure on the part of the states to make a viable legal argument that the public lands belonged to them. Reagan opposed environmentalism in every possible way— by dismissing acid rain (a form of pollution that destroyed fish and plant life in many Canadian and American lakes throughout the 1970s) and by weakening the EPA with corrupt administrators and a withered budget.

By 1990, being green no longer had the same meaning that it had in 1970. *Ecofeminist* theory (thinking about gender and nature together as the context for understanding male-dominated culture) and the *Gaia hypothesis* (proposed by British scientist James Lovelock, positing the earth as a single organism), both formulated during the 1970s and 1980s, were important intellectual achievements for environmentalists, but they alienated the general public. At the same time, however, the consumption aesthetic of environmentalists seemed to rise in public esteem. *Organic Style* magazine and the Whole Foods supermarket chain reflected a desire for pure food and simple living without making demands on consumers to reduce the quantity of their consumption. Corporations found it effortless to advertise their products as "environmentally friendly" even if they were not, thus asking the public to believe (in one example) that oil extraction did no harm to wildlife. This tactic of corporate "greenwashing" played into the public's desire for value-free consumption. Yet this new form of green living belonged to the privileged—those who could afford lifestyle changes.

ALL ENVIRONMENTALISM IS LOCAL

In 1974, Lois Gibbs moved to the neighborhood of Love Canal, New York, not far from Niagara Falls, with her husband and her one-year-old son. Four years later, her son developed severe asthma, followed by a blood disease and convulsions. Her daughter, born at Love Canal, was diagnosed with the same disease. Around that time, Gibbs read an article in the local paper about chemicals buried under her children's school and immediately requested the transfer of her children. The Board of Education refused even to acknowledge the problem, so she organized a neighborhood group to demand that the school close. She was twenty-seven years old.

The 20,000 tons of chemicals seeping under the Gibbs' neighborhood came from the Hooker Chemical Corporation, which had dumped them in an abandoned canal owned by the city. The company used the site for decades before 1953, when it covered the canal and sold it to the Board of Education for one dollar. Hooker claimed afterward that it had warned the Board not to disturb the site and refused responsibility for any harm or death caused by the chemicals buried there. Meanwhile, a developer had purchased land nearby and built a neighborhood. Unaware of these events, residents had moved in during the 1950s and 1960s and had immediately begun complaining about nausea and burns on their skin (Document 28).

Like industrial waste itself, the history of dumping at Love Canal was meant to be forgotten. No one took the complaints of residents seriously until the 1970s, when residents demanded that the state or federal government purchase their houses so that they could leave and get on with their lives. After years of hearings, letters, protests, and coverage in the local newspaper, during which time scientists warned residents not to eat vegetables from their gardens or enter the basements of their houses, President Jimmy Carter declared Love Canal a disaster area. In 1980, as Carter left office, Congress appropriated $17 million for the emergency relocation of Love Canal families, mostly to purchase their houses, and passed the Superfund Law to finance the cleanup of future toxic disasters. Today, there are about 1,500 Superfund sites nationwide.

The story of Love Canal is a story about toxicity and the inequalities of class. Wealthy people do not want refineries or chemical dumps anywhere near where they live. Poor people endure these hazards, and sometimes live with a shocking level of toxicity from polluted air and water. After World War II, a landscape of poverty emerged that could be overlaid with astonishing congruence on any map of waste sites and emissions streams. Although the residents of Love Canal did not live in poverty, they still did not have the money to leave their houses behind and flee to a place where they could live safely. During the crisis, residents insisted that their houses represented all of their savings, so the destruction of the value of their property represented an illegal "taking" by the company responsible for dumping the chemicals. Like poor people in cities and refugee camps all over the world, they were trapped in an environment that was killing them.

Love Canal is also a story about environmentalism. Gibbs and her neighbors acted without the help of any of the major environmental organizations, none of which recognized toxic chemicals in drinking water as an "environmental" problem. Until very recently, it would have been impossible to argue that environmentalism could become a social movement, even though reformers have observed the obvious relationships between poverty and noxious environments since the nineteenth century, when epidemics caused by unsanitary drinking water ravaged immigrant neighborhoods such as New York's Five

Points. White middle-class men and women who joined the Sierra Club in the 1940s tended to look past cities to fix their gaze on "unspoiled" mountains and deserts. Like conservation, environmentalism had mostly been the concern of people who had never suffered racial prejudice or worried that leaders in government would ignore their complaints. The importance of Love Canal is that it fused social and environmental concerns and made it impossible for anyone to ignore the obvious confluence of economic hardship, toxicity, and sickness.

The movement for environmental justice argues that a clean environment—at work and at home—is a human right. This final layer of environmentalism at the local level is the one that is most vital and vibrant today. Wilma Subra, a chemist and citizen, has worked with more than 500 communities, most along an eighty-five-mile stretch of the lower Mississippi River known as "Cancer Alley," to identify and analyze their sources of toxic pollution. Chemical factories and refineries pump tens of millions of pounds of pollutants into the river each year in areas where poor African Americans live. Subra lobbies the Louisiana legislature so ceaselessly that its members know her by name; she confronts companies with the consequences of their practices; and she helps the residents cope. Other activists for environmental justice include Vernice D. Miller, cofounder of West Harlem Environmental Action (Document 30); the late César Chávez, founder of the United Farm Workers (Document 29); and Dana Alston, who helped organize the First National People of Color Environmental Leadership Summit in October 1991. Alston addressed representatives of the major environmental organizations, telling them: "For us, the issues of the environment do not stand alone by themselves. They are not narrowly defined. Our vision of the environment is woven into an overall framework of social, racial and economic justice. . . . The environment, for us, is where we live, where we work and where we play."[12]

CONCLUSION: PITFALLS AND POSSIBILITIES

Environmentalism has not figured prominently in any presidency since Richard Nixon's, nor has any candidate for national office made it central to his or her campaign, including Al Gore. Gore wrote *Earth in the Balance: Ecology and the Human Spirit* while serving as U.S. senator from Tennessee and before becoming vice president under Bill Clinton in 1992. *Earth in the Balance* remains the most thoughtful and comprehensive essay about the environment ever written by an elected official, and Gore clearly intended it to carve out a centrist position that he could use for a run at the presidency. But he abandoned his own conclusions during his 2000 campaign, fearful that Republicans, led by George W. Bush, would use the issue against him. In that change of strategy lies the present state of environmentalism. Rather than make his own case for protection with continued growth, Gore let the opposition define the environment as an economic threat. For regardless of the air quality improved; the rivers cleaned; the beaches restored; the whales saved; the chemicals banned; the parks created; the wilderness preserved; and the children taught to reduce, reuse, and recycle, many Americans feel apprehensive that environmentalism poses a threat to economic growth.[13]

Yet Americans have continued to recognize environmental decline and the need to reverse it. Though environmentalism now has few allies among national politicians, people place the environment high on their list of concerns. One poll, taken in March 2005, revealed that 63 percent of Americans thought that the environment was getting worse, 50 percent thought that President George W. Bush had done too little to improve it, and 49 percent thought that it should be given priority over economic growth.[14] In 2001, a federation of state "green parties" joined the Green Party of the United States. The Greens emphasize democracy, community organization, and economic and gender equality. Consumer advocate Ralph Nader ran for president as their candidate in 1996 and again in 2000, when he won 2.7 percent of the vote.

The earth, its human cultures, and all its forms of life are as fragile now as they first seemed after the first nuclear weapons incinerated the people of Hiroshima and Nagasaki. But while the threat to life in 1946 came from a single cataclysmic source in the hands of one government, the threat today comes from billions of people engaged in economic activity that places them in streams of carbon emissions. The conflicting political and economic interests involved in confronting climate change came into view after the Kyoto Protocol in 1997. The United States all but ignored the agreement, refusing to ratify it. In response to growing scientific evidence that carbon emissions contributed to climate change and the urging of constituents, Senators John McCain (R-Ariz.) and Joseph Lieberman (D-Conn.) introduced the Climate Stewardship Act, legislation that would have controlled emissions from the United States for the first time.

The bill proposed to reduce carbon dioxide and other emissions to 2000 levels by the year 2010—a more modest goal than what the assembled nations agreed upon at Kyoto. In 2004, the Senate rejected the bill by a vote of 43 to 55. Though its sponsors have vowed to bring it back, the defeat of the Climate Stewardship Act suggests the distance between the problem and any political solution. Environmentalists and many scientists complain that public policy lags far behind the true urgency of the problem; other critics note that environmentalism as it existed into the 1980s is no longer a visible influence over government or public opinion. Perhaps the most difficult question has to do with the electorate and its shifting priorities since the 1970s. When the national security of Americans includes the security of a safe and equitable environment in North America and throughout the world, there will be a new environmental politics.

NOTES

[1]John T. Cumbler, *Reasonable Use: The People, the Environment, and the State, New England 1790–1930* (New York: Oxford University Press, 2001).

[2]John Muir, *My First Summer in the Sierra* (1911), chap. 5: The Yosemite.

[3]John Muir, *The Yosemite* (New York: Century Co., 1912), Chap. 16, http://www.yosemite.ca.us/john_muir_writings. Retrieved April 14, 2006.

[4]For more on this subject, see Mark W. T. Harvey, *A Symbol of Wilderness: Echo Park and the American Conservation Movement* (Albuquerque: University of New Mexico Press, 1994).

[5]For more about how the 1960s shaped the environmental movement, see Adam Rome, "'Give Earth a Chance': The Environmental Movement and the Sixties," *Journal of American History* 90 (September 2003): 525–54.

[6]For more on environmental economics, see Herman E. Daly, *Steady-State Economics* (San Francisco: W. H. Freeman and Company, 1977), and Robert L. Nadeau, *The Wealth of Nature: How Mainstream Economics Has Failed the Environment* (New York: Columbia University Press, 2003).

[7]*UN 1990 Long-Term Predictions and UN 1994 Revised Projections*, as reported by the United States Global Change Research Information Office, www.gcrio.org. Retrieved April 17, 2006. Also see Carl Haub, *The UN Long-Range Population Projections: What They Tell Us* (Washington, D.C.: Population Reference Bureau, Inc., 1992).

[8]Ernst Haeckel makes this statement in *The Evolution of Man* (1879), vol. 1, chap. 1.5: The Modern Science of Evolution.

[9]For the best recent example of historical ecology, see David R. Foster and John D. Aber, eds., *Forests in Time: The Environmental Consequences of 1,000 Years of Change in New England* (New Haven, Conn.: Yale University Press, 2004).

[10]For these and other statistics, see http://yosemite.epa.gov/oar/globalwarming.nsf/content/Climate.html (May 3, 2005).

[11]E. F. Schumacher, *Small Is Beautiful: A Study of Economics as If People Mattered* (London: Blond and Briggs, 1973).

[12]Dana Alston, "Moving beyond the Barriers," reprinted from Charles Lee, ed., "The First National People of Color Environmental Leadership Summit: Proceedings" (New York: United Church of Christ Commission for Racial Justice, 1992).

[13]A similar list is found in Michael Shellenberger and Ted Nordhaus, *The Death of Environmentalism: Global Warming Politics in a Post-Environmental World* (2004), http://www.thebreakthrough.org/images/Death_of_Environmentalism.pdf.

[14]The last statistic is from a poll taken in March 2004; the others are from March 2005. All can be found in The Gallup Polls or at http://www.pollingreport.com (July 2005).

PART TWO

The Documents

1

Wilderness Romanticism

1

ANSEL ADAMS

Clearing Winter Storm

1944

Ansel Adams visited the Yosemite Valley with his family in 1916 and soon began taking pictures of it (see page 30). He worked as a commercial photographer for thirty years. During that time, he emerged as the preeminent wilderness photographer of the twentieth century, creating images that evoked the same feelings of awe and inspiration that romantic painters and writers had sought to create a century before. Once Adams became a board member of the Sierra Club, his photographs took on a more pointed purpose: to inspire people who might never visit wilderness to join the organization and give money to its political action funds.

Clearing Winter Storm (1944), Photograph by Ansel Adams. Collection Center for Creative Photography, University of Arizona.

Clearing Winter Storm

In this majestic photograph of Yosemite National Park, Adams conveys the strength and power of the natural world.

2

MARJORY STONEMAN DOUGLAS

The Everglades

1947

Working as an assistant editor at the Miami Herald *during the 1920s, Marjory Stoneman Douglas began to write about the condition of the Florida Everglades. She published* The Everglades: River of Grass *in 1947 to bring its history and ecology to a popular audience and to build support for its preservation. The book is a loving tribute to the interdependence of the organisms and landscapes that make up the giant wetland between Lake Okeechobee and the mangroves at the southern tip of Florida. Douglas addressed a reading public more inclined to consider the Everglades a giant swamp than to imagine it on an equal footing with Yellowstone or Yosemite national parks. In 1932, she urged Congress to designate the Everglades as a national park, which Congress finally did in 1947.*

There are no other Everglades in the world.

They are, they have always been, one of the unique regions of the earth, remote, never wholly known. Nothing anywhere else is like them: their vast glittering openness, wider than the enormous visible round of the horizon, the racing free saltness and sweetness of their massive winds, under the dazzling blue heights of space. They are unique also in the simplicity, the diversity, the related harmony of the forms of life they enclose. The miracle of the light pours over the green and brown expanse of saw grass and of water, shining and slow-moving below, the grass and water that is the meaning and the central fact of the Everglades of Florida. It is a river of grass.

The great pointed paw of the state of Florida, familiar as the map of North America itself, of which it is the most noticeable appendage, thrusts south, farther south than any other part of the mainland of the

Marjory Stoneman Douglas, *The Everglades: River of Grass* (New York: Rinehart, 1947), 5–6, 9–10, 349–50, 374–76.

United States. Between the shining aquamarine waters of the Gulf of
Mexico and the roaring deep-blue waters of the north-surging Gulf
Stream, the shaped land points toward Cuba and the Caribbean. It
points toward and touches within one degree of the tropics.

More than halfway down that thrusting sea-bound peninsula nearly
everyone knows the lake that is like a great hole in that pawing shape,
Lake Okeechobee, the second largest body of fresh water, it is always
said, "within the confines of the United States." Below that lie the
Everglades.

They have been called "the mysterious Everglades" so long that the
phrase is a meaningless platitude. For four hundred years after the
discovery they seemed more like a fantasy than a simple geographic
and historic fact. Even the men who in the later years saw them more
clearly could hardly make up their minds what the Everglades were or
how they could be described, or what use could be made of them.
They were mysterious then. They are mysterious still to everyone by
whom their fundamental nature is not understood. . . .

The Everglades begin at Lake Okeechobee.

That is the name later Indians gave the lake, a name almost
as recent as the word "Everglades." It means "Big Water." Everybody
knows it.

Yet few have any idea of those pale, seemingly illimitable waters.
Over the shallows, often less than a foot deep but seven hundred fifty
or so square miles in actual area, the winds in one gray swift moment
can shatter the reflections of sky and cloud whiteness standing still in
that shining, polished, shimmering expanse. A boat can push for
hours in a day of white sun through the short, crisp lake waves and
there will be nothing to be seen anywhere but the brightness where
the color of the water and the color of the sky become one. Men out of
sight of land can stand in it up to their armpits and slowly "walk in"
their long nets to the waiting boats. An everglade kite and his mate,
questing in great solitary circles, rising and dipping and rising again
on the wind currents, can look down all day long at the water faintly
green with floating water lettuce or marked by thin standing lines of
reeds, utter their sharp goat cries, and be seen and heard by no one
at all.

There are great shallow islands, all brown reeds or shrubby trees
thick in the water. There are masses of water weeds and hyacinths
and flags rooted so long they seem solid earth, yet there is nothing
but lake bottom to stand on. There the egret and the white ibis and

the glossy ibis and the little blue herons in their thousands nested and circled and fed.

A long northeast wind, a "norther," can lash all that still surface to dirty vicious gray and white, over which the rain mists shut down like stained rolls of wool, so that from the eastern sand rim under dripping cypresses or the west ridge with its live oaks, no one would guess that all that waste of empty water stretched there but for the long monotonous wash of waves on unseen marshy shores.

Saw grass reaches up both sides of that lake in great enclosing arms, so that it is correct to say that the Everglades are there also. But south, southeast and southwest, where the lake water slopped and seeped and ran over and under the rock and soil, the greatest mass of the saw grass begins. It stretches as it always has stretched, in one thick enormous curving river of grass, to the very end. This is the Everglades.

It reaches one hundred miles from Lake Okeechobee to the Gulf of Mexico, fifty, sixty, even seventy miles wide. No one has ever fought his way along its full length. Few have ever crossed the northern wilderness of nothing but grass. Down that almost invisible slope the water moves. The grass stands. Where the grass and the water are there is the heart, the current, the meaning of the Everglades.

The grass and the water together make the river as simple as it is unique. There is no other river like it. . . .

The Everglades were dying.

The endless acres of saw grass, brown as an enormous shadow where rain and lake water had once flowed, rustled dry. The birds flew high above them, the ibis, the egret, the heron beating steadily southward along drying watercourses to the last brackish pools. Fires that one night glittered along a narrow horizon the next day, before a racing wind, flashed crackling and roaring across the grassy world and flamed up in rolling columns of yellow smoke like pillars of dirty clouds.

Perhaps the wind dropped and a quick rain came and put out the fire that had moved too fast to burn deep. Where it had spread its blackness the saw grass had thrust up its green again, thinly, in drier muck. The insects shrilled. The sun blazed. But in all the creatures of those solitudes where the Tamiami Trail and the long canals stretched their thin lines, and in the hearts of the Indians, there was a sense of evil abroad, a restlessness, an anxiety that one passing rainfall could not change.

The cities did not feel it.

Miami rejoiced, after the depression, in its increasing growth. It grew as great cities seem to grow, as if there were places and times in which human activity becomes a whirlpool which gathers force, not only from man's courage and ambitions but from the very tides of disaster and human foolishness that otherwise disperse them. It grew almost in spite of the mistakes of its people, by some power which puts to work good and bad, fineness and cheapness, everything, so long as it has fiber and force and the aliveness that makes more life. Miami grew with the tough thrust and vigor of a tropical organism. Its strength was that nothing human was foreign to it. . . .

The saw grass dried, rustling like paper. Garfish, thick in the pools where there had been watercourses, ate all the other fish, and died and stank in their thousands. The birds flew over and far south, searching for fresh water. The lower pools shrank and were brackish. Deer and raccoons traveled far, losing their fear of houses and people in their increasing thirst.

The fires began.

Cattlemen's grass fires roared uncontrolled. Cane-field fires spread crackling and hissing in the saw grass in vast waves and pillars and blowing mountains of heavy, cream-colored, purple-shadowed smoke. Training planes flying over the Glades dropped bombs or cigarette butts, and the fires exploded in the hearts of the drying hammocks and raced on before every wind leaving only blackness. Palmetto burst in the fiery heat that spread from pine tree to pine tree in flaming brands. The flames ate down into the drying ancient saw-grass muck and smoldered and burned and glowed there for weeks, slow orange glares in the night or constant rolling smoke by day, eating down to the ultimate rock.

The acrid smoke drifted over the cities, and people choked and suffocated in it. Many left.

Men watching from fire towers got tired of counting smokes against which they could do nothing. There was no water in the canals with which to fight them. Houses, trees, groves, were burned. The fires swept along the Tamiami Trail and burned the camps as the Indians fled from them. There were weeks when the trail and the other roads were closed to traffic, blinded by the dense covering choking smoke.

All night long the fires stood about the sky, their glare as high as the sky, the flames reflected on the churning orange pillars of their smoke. And when in the daytime they had passed slowly, burning and glowing down to the rock, behind them was only the blackness of desolation.

The whole Everglades were burning. What had been a river of grass and sweet water that had given meaning and life and uniqueness to this whole enormous geography through centuries in which man had no place here was made, in one chaotic gesture of greed and ignorance and folly, a river of fire.

Then, all the people of the cities who had not paid much attention to the Everglades were startled by another thing. The sweet water the rock had held was gone or had shrunk down far into its strange holes and cleavages. The rim of the rock, which in perfect balance had established the life of the Glades, had also held back the salty unending power of the sea. Now the tides moved easily up through the cuts and breaks men had dynamited in the rocky eastern retaining walls. The heavy salt water crept up the rivers and to their headwaters and beyond, up the canals and the least drying watercourses.

The salt water invaded the land, 230 feet a year in the first years, and then faster, spreading through banks and soil 890 feet, nearly 1,000 feet a year. It invaded the wells in all the porous rock rim eastward and invaded the rock itself where the old sweet springs had dried long since. The salt penetrated the soil of the tomato prairies, and the strawberry lands up the Miami River. Wells in southeastern groves turned brackish and the salt stayed in the soil as the groves died. With no rain, the salt was not leached out. The Homestead well field, where the new pipeline went to the keys and Key West, was endangered. The salt water moved into the well field of the city of Miami, far above where the rapids had once guarded the Glades from the sea.

In the Glades the fires raged. Up the rivers and the canals, through the rock and the soil, across the lowlands not much higher than high tide, the salt worked. . . .

In a week in which the fires spread into the drying jungles, flashed across the firebreaks, the flames worked and smoldered deep in the roots and hearts of the beautiful old live oaks. All the fine tropical trees of the jungle were eaten out. Birds, snakes, deer, small animals were caught in the flames. The delicate tree snails were burned, the orchids, the air plants, the ancient leather ferns, the butterflies. What had been unique and lovely and strange was a black monotony of destruction.

3

THE SIERRA CLUB

The Defense of Dinosaur

1954

Thirty years after the flood waters claimed the Hetch Hetchy Valley, members of the Sierra Club understood the significance of the Bureau of Reclamation's plan to place dams at various points within the drainage of the Colorado River. The controversy broke in the February 1954 issue of the Sierra Club Bulletin. *Previous editions had featured mountaineering expeditions, topographical mapping, and a philosophical discourse on the value of wilderness, but February sounded an alarm: "Trouble in Dinosaur. . . . URGENT: Please read this issue now—and lend a hand" (page 37). Articles in the issue made explicit comparisons between the threat to Dinosaur National Monument and the fate of Hetch Hetchy, including before and after photographs showing the granite-walled California valley turned into "a drab reservoir." This excerpt is from that February issue and was written either by Dick Leonard, Sierra Club president, or by David Brower, its executive director. The articles represented the first time since John Muir's efforts that the Sierra Club or any organization of wilderness enthusiasts attempted to mobilize for a political cause.*

Opposite: *Sierra Club on Alert*

This issue of the *Sierra Club Bulletin* announced that a federal water-storage project would flood Dinosaur National Monument, a part of the national park system. It also revealed new interest in political action to preserve wilderness. From the cover of *Sierra Club Bulletin* (February 1954). Used by permission from Martin Litton and Sierra Club Books.

Sierra Club Bulletin (February 1954), 3–9.

SIERRA CLUB
BULLETIN

February 1954

RAINBOW RECESS, YAMPA RIVER, DINOSAUR NATIONAL MONUMENT

Trouble in Dinosaur

The rainbow canyons of the Yampa and the Green, corridors through a primitive paradise unequalled anywhere, are a unique gem of the National Park System. They are now needlessly threatened. You can prevent their destruction. Men of vision saved this place for us. Now it's turnabout.

URGENT: Please read this issue now—and lend a hand.

THE WILDERNESS SOCIETY SENDS YOU THIS ISSUE
TO STRESS THE URGENT NEED TO ACT PROMPLY

Two Wasteful Dams—Or a Great National Park?

Interior Secretary McKay is pressing for speedy authorization for Echo Park Dam, which would destroy the park value of the canyons of Dinosaur National Monument. He has asked for later construction of Split Mountain dam, which would compound the destruction. He describes the Upper Colorado Storage Project, of which these dams are presently a part, as a bold plan to fill an urgent need. Sparing Dinosaur, he has concluded, would be wasteful; the dams, he says, won't hurt the scenery much.

The project is bold, yes; it will take more than a billion dollars to start it.

But are these two dams urgently needed? Are they needed at all[?] *Absolutely not.*

Hetch Hetchy Valley once had a setting. Now it has a drab reservoir, water for a city that could still get it elsewhere.

What will they do to the scenery? The Park Service report says, the effects upon "irreplaceable . . . values of national significance would be deplorable."

Would alternate damsites, which Mr. McKay knows exist, be wasteful? We don't know, and he doesn't know. He has been rushed into accepting a not-very-well-educated guess; his recommendation, based on that guess, may itself be a needless waste of nearly eighty million dollars of our money; his recommendation, enacted, would ruin forever one of the finest scenic and recreational assets in the National Park System, which he is charged by law with protecting.

This attack on the Park System comes at the head of Reclamation's agenda. Yet the entire bold Upper Colorado Project, according to the Bureau's own guess, will not be fully utilized for seventy-five years. And while the various dams sit there, awaiting their full utilization, they'll gather enough silt to cover the entire state of New Hampshire more than a foot deep (100,000 acre-feet per year—Bureau of Reclamation figure).

The Secretary of Agriculture worries about surpluses; the upper Colorado Basin is now exporting power; various alternate combinations will store the water and produce the power. Even if these things weren't true, there'd be no logical reason for the rush to ruin Dinosaur with an Echo Park dam as first rattle out of the box.

Then what is the hurry? *That*, as the man said, is a good question. This rush is the opposite of good conservation. Either we stop it, or we prepare to watch men of little vision whittle away the century's gains in conservation—and we turn our heads while Theodore Roosevelt turns in his grave.

Conservationists across the land—and Interior's National Park Service, before it was silenced—agree with the following stand:

1. Dinosaur National Monument is an outstanding part of the National Park System, which the people, through their Congress, have been diligent to protect since its creation, and should protect today.

2. The proposed Echo Park and Split Mountain dams would destroy the park value of Dinosaur; the unique would give way to the commonplace and would imperil the entire Park System.

3. The water and power needs of the Upper Basin states for the foreseeable future can be adequately accommodated without invading the National Park System.

Dinosaur belongs to the people—all of them, not just a few. The people—you, your neighbor, his neighbor—are thoroughly capable of saving it if they act promptly, concertedly, and wisely, letting their Congress know that they don't want it given away, even if the engineering reasons are plausible.

For the Defense of Dinosaur—An Outline

1. a) *The threat is real and immediate.* The enemy of conservation, in Dinosaur, is primarily lack of vision and an absence of appreciation of intangible values. Local people have so thoroughly convinced themselves that Echo Park dam is essential that great political pressure has been built up. Legislation calling for the dam was introduced last year; hearings started in the House January 18, to continue through the week of the 25th. Every effort is being made to rush the bills through before opposition to Echo Park dam builds up.

b) *Conservation organizations all over the country are aroused* and are acting in unison. Strong editorial support, cutting across party lines, has come from most parts of the country in response to an alerting call that came inevitably late, and includes the New York *Times*, San Francisco *Chronicle*, Los Angeles *Times*, Coconino *Sun*, Washington *Post*, and the Knoxville *Journal*. Among the magazines scheduling

Dinosaur stories are *Harper's, National Geographic, The Reporter, Sunset, Pacific Discovery*. President Eisenhower has stated that it is his intention to protect "national forests, parks, monuments, and other natural and historic sites. . . ."

2. *The one mission of all conservationists*: to keep Dinosaur National Monument unimpaired as an important part of a world-renowned National Park System. A secondary objective is to create a full-fledged national park in Dinosaur, giving it the increased prestige it unquestionably merits. Legislation to make it a park was introduced last year; no hearings are scheduled yet.

3. *To accomplish this mission*, organizations with conservation programs and individuals with conservation ideals must immediately urge their Congressmen to protect the National Park System, and must rapidly become well enough informed about the Dinosaur details to meet head-on the allegations of the dam proponents.

4. Use all the methods of communication you can arrange for. Let your organizations know—*if* you have time to—what you're doing to help.

5. *You*, and the effort you make today as an individual, are the key to the defense of Dinosaur—and to making it the full-fledged National Park it should be.

Gist of the Claims—The Truth as We See It

CLAIM: Few people see the Dinosaur canyons; they're too inaccessible.

TRUTH: A modest appropriation would correct this and permit conservative improvement of existing roads. So far Dinosaur has been appropriation-starved. Mr. McKay has asked for $21 million for study and development of what remains of the Monument after destruction by damming. A small fraction of this would be more than adequate for access and facilities if Dinosaur is saved. Moreover, people have only just begun to learn how easy, safe, thrilling, unique, and inexpensive it is to travel Dinosaur's wilderness river trails—the Yampa and the Green—by boat.

CLAIM: The dams won't destroy Dinosaur, and won't drown the Dinosaur quarry.

TRUTH: 99% wrong and 1% correct. The quarry is worthwhile and safe; but compared to the canyons, it is scenically insignificant. The dams would devastate the park value of the canyons; he who would claim otherwise just doesn't understand what a national park is all about. In the words of the National Park Report, the effect of the dam on irreplaceable park values would be deplorable. The Echo Park project entails: a dam 525 feet high, 107 miles of reservoir inundating more than 300 square miles with six million plus acre feet of water, construction roads in the canyons, tunnels, power installation and transmission lines, constant build-up of silt, and periodic drawdowns of the reservoir. "Deplorable" is a mild word to describe what this would do to any national monument, and to these canyons in particular.

CLAIM: More people can see the canyons by boating in the reservoirs.

TRUTH: "Yes, you can look at part of the setting—after we've lost the priceless gem." It's a little like that. These canyons and rivers are unique, irreplaceable; reservoirs are neither, they are fine enough in their place. Utah and Colorado can have both—their reservoirs and an unspoiled Dinosaur for the world.

4

WALLACE STEGNER

Wilderness Letter

1960

Before President Lyndon Johnson signed the Wilderness Act in 1964, wilderness did not exist as a distinct land use in the United States. For almost a century, national parks had offered visitors easy access to once remote places such as Yosemite Valley and the Grand Canyon, including services such as hotels, campgrounds, guided tours, and scenic roads. But a rising generation of wilderness advocates wanted something different—places where they could experience primitive conditions, where the imprint of society would not be evident in the landscape. The writer Wallace Stegner wrote this letter to David Pesonen of the Wildland Research Center at the University of California to argue for the spiritual value of wilderness, for its importance to children, as a salve to "our insane lives," and for its role in shaping American history. The letter became

Wallace Stegner, *The Sound of Mountain Water: The Changing American West* (New York: Doubleday, 1969), 145–55.

*part of a report submitted by the Outdoor Recreation Resources Review
Commission in support of the bill, then under debate in Congress, that
would become the Wilderness Act.*

Dear Mr. Pesonen:

I believe that you are working on the wilderness portion of the Outdoor Recreation Resources Review Commission's report. If I may, I
should like to urge some arguments for wilderness preservation that
involve recreation, as it is ordinarily conceived, hardly at all. Hunting,
fishing, hiking, mountain-climbing, camping, photography, and the
enjoyment of natural scenery will all, surely, figure in your report. So
will the wilderness as a genetic reserve, a scientific yardstick by
which we may measure the world in its natural balance against the
world in its man-made imbalance. What I want to speak for is not so
much the wilderness uses, valuable as those are, but the wilderness
idea, which is a resource in itself. Being an intangible and spiritual
resource, it will seem mystical to the practical minded—but then anything that cannot be moved by a bulldozer is likely to seem mystical to
them.

I want to speak for the wilderness idea as something that has
helped form our character and that has certainly shaped our history
as a people. It has no more to do with recreation than churches have
to do with recreation, or than the strenuousness and optimism and
expansiveness of what the historians call the "American Dream" have
to do with recreation. Nevertheless, since it is only in this recreation
survey that the values of wilderness are being compiled, I hope you
will permit me to insert this idea between the leaves, as it were, of the
recreation report.

Something will have gone out of us as a people if we ever let the
remaining wilderness be destroyed; if we permit the last virgin forests
to be turned into comic books and plastic cigarette cases; if we drive
the few remaining members of the wild species into zoos or to extinction; if we pollute the last clear air and dirty the last clean streams and
push our paved roads through the last of the silence, so that never
again will Americans be free in their own country from the noise, the
exhausts, the stinks of human and automotive waste. And so that
never again can we have the chance to see ourselves single, separate,
vertical and individual in the world, part of the environment of trees

and rocks and soil, brother to the other animals, part of the natural world and competent to belong in it. Without any remaining wilderness we are committed wholly, without chance for even momentary reflection and rest, to a headlong drive into our technological termite-life, the Brave New World of a completely man-controlled environment. We need wilderness preserved—as much of it as is still left, and as many kinds—because it was the challenge against which our character as a people was formed. The reminder and the reassurance that it is still there is good for our spiritual health even if we never once in ten years set foot in it. It is good for us when we are young, because of the incomparable sanity it can bring briefly, as vacation and rest, into our insane lives. It is important to us when we are old simply because it is there—important, that is, simply as an idea.

We are a wild species, as Darwin pointed out. Nobody ever tamed or domesticated or scientifically bred us. But for at least three millennia we have been engaged in a cumulative and ambitious race to modify and gain control of our environment, and in the process we have come close to domesticating ourselves. Not many people are likely, any more, to look upon what we call "progress" as an unmixed blessing. Just as surely as it has brought us increased comfort and more material goods, it has brought us spiritual losses, and it threatens now to become the Frankenstein that will destroy us. One means of sanity is to retain a hold on the natural world, to remain, insofar as we can, good animals. Americans still have that chance, more than many peoples; for while we were demonstrating ourselves the most efficient and ruthless environment-busters in history, and slashing and burning and cutting our way through a wilderness continent, the wilderness was working on us. It remains in us as surely as Indian names remain on the land. If the abstract dream of human liberty and human dignity became, in America, something more than an abstract dream, mark it down at least partially to the fact that we were in subdued ways subdued by what we conquered. . . .

Even when I can't get to the back country, the thought of the colored deserts of southern Utah, or the reassurance that there are still stretches of prairies where the world can be instantaneously perceived as disk and bowl, and where the little but intensely important human being is exposed to the five directions of the thirty-six winds, is a positive consolation. The idea alone can sustain me. But as the wilderness areas are progressively exploited or "improve," as the jeeps and bulldozers of uranium prospectors scar up the deserts and the roads are cut into the alpine timberlands, and as the remnants of the unspoiled and natural world are progressively eroded, every such loss is a little death in me. In us.

I am not moved by the argument that those wilderness areas which have already been exposed to grazing or mining are already deflowered, and so might as well be "harvested." For mining I cannot say much good except that its operations are generally short-lived. The extractable wealth is taken and the shafts, the tailings, and the ruins left, and in a dry country such as the American West the wounds men make in the earth do not quickly heal. Still, they are only wounds; they aren't absolutely mortal. Better a wounded wilderness than none at all. And as for grazing, if it is strictly controlled so that it does not destroy the ground cover, damage the ecology, or compete with the wildlife it is in itself nothing that need conflict with the wilderness feeling or the validity of the wilderness experience. I have known enough range cattle to recognize them as wild animals; and the people who herd them have, in the wilderness context, the dignity of rareness; they belong on the frontier, moreover, and have a look of rightness. The invasion they make on the virgin country is a sort of invasion that is as old as Neolithic man, and they can, in moderation, even emphasize a man's feeling of belonging to the natural world. Under surveillance, they can belong; under control, they need not deface or mar. I do not believe that in wilderness areas where grazing has never been permitted, it should be permitted; but I do not believe either that an otherwise untouched wilderness should be eliminated from the preservation plan because of limited existing uses such as grazing which are in consonance with the frontier condition and image.

Let me say something on the subject of the kinds of wilderness worth preserving. Most of those areas contemplated are in the national forests and in high mountain country. For all the usual recreational purposes, the alpine and the forest wildernesses are obviously the most important, both as genetic banks and as beauty spots. But for the spiritual renewal, the recognition of identity, the birth of awe, other kinds will serve every bit as well. Perhaps, because they are less friendly to life, more abstractly nonhuman, they will serve even better. On our Saskatchewan prairie, the nearest neighbor was four miles away, and at night we saw only two lights on all the dark rounding earth. The earth was full of animals—field mice, ground squirrels, weasels, ferrets, badgers, coyotes, burrowing owls, snakes. I knew them as my little brothers, as fellow creatures, and I have never been able to look upon animals in any other way since. The sky in that country came clear down to the ground on every side, and it was full of great weathers, and clouds, and winds, and hawks. I hope I learned something from looking a long way, from looking up, from being much alone. A prairie like that, one big enough to carry the eye clear to the sinking, rounding horizon, can be as lonely and grand and simple in its forms as the sea. It is as good a place as any for the wilderness experience to happen; the vanishing prairie is as worth preserving for the wilderness idea as the alpine forest.

So are great reaches of our western deserts, scarred somewhat by prospectors but otherwise open, beautiful, waiting, close to whatever God you want to see in them. Just as a sample, let me suggest the Robbers' Roost country in Wayne County, Utah, near the Capitol Reef National Monument. In that desert climate the dozer and jeep tracks will not soon melt back into the earth, but the country has a way of making the scars insignificant. It is a lovely and terrible wilderness, such as wilderness as Christ and the prophets went out into; harshly and beautifully colored, broken and worn until its bones are exposed, its great sky without a smudge of taint from Technocracy, and in hidden corners and pockets under its cliffs the sudden poetry of springs. Save a piece of country like that intact, and it does not matter in the slightest that only a few people every year will go into it. That is precisely its value. Roads would be a desecration, crowds would ruin it. But those who haven't the strength or youth to go into it and live can simply sit and look. They can look two hundred miles, clear into Colorado: and looking down over the cliffs and canyons of the San Rafael Swell and the Robbers' Roost they can also look as deeply into themselves as anywhere I know. And if they can't even get to the places on the Aquarius Plateau where the present roads will carry them, they can simply contemplate the idea, take pleasure in the fact that such a timeless and uncontrolled part of earth is still there.

These are some of the things wilderness can do for us. That is the reason we need to put into effect, for its preservation, some other principle than the principles of exploitation or "usefulness" or even recreation. We simply need that wild country available to us, even if we never do more than drive to its edge and look in. For it can be a means of reassuring ourselves of our sanity as creatures, a part of the geography of hope.

Very sincerely yours,
Wallace Stegner

5

DAVID BROWER

The Place No One Knew
1963

In 1956, environmentalists, led by the Sierra Club, agreed to withdraw their opposition to the Colorado River Storage project — including a dam across Glen Canyon — if the Bureau of Reclamation agreed to remove the Echo Park dam from its agenda. David Brower regretted the agreement soon after it was concluded. In 1963, Brower eulogized Glen Canyon in the foreword to The Place No One Knew, *a photographic essay created in the months before the floodwaters rose up against the canyon's sandstone walls.*

Glen Canyon died in 1963 and I was partly responsible for its needless death. So were you. Neither you nor I, nor anyone else, knew it well enough to insist that at all costs it should endure. When we began to find out it was too late. On January 21, 1963, the last day on which the execution of one of the planet's greatest scenic antiquities could yet have been stayed, the man who theoretically had the power to save this place did not find a way to pick up a telephone and give the necessary order. I was within a few feet of his desk in Washington that day and witnessed how the forces long at work finally had their way. So a steel gate dropped, choking off the flow in the canyon's carotid artery, and from that moment the canyon's life force ebbed quickly. A huge reservoir, absolutely not needed in this century, almost certainly not needed in the next, and conceivably never to be needed at all, began to fill. At this writing the rising waters are destined to blot out everything of beauty which this book records. . . .

The best of the canyon is going or gone. Some second-best beauty remains along the Colorado of course, but much of its meaning vanished when Glen Canyon died. The rest will go the way Glen Canyon did unless enough people begin to feel uneasy about the current inter-

David Brower, "Foreword," in Eliot Porter, *The Place No One Knew: Glen Canyon on the Colorado* (San Francisco: Sierra Club Books, 1963), 7–9.

pretation of what progress consists of—unless they are willing to ask if progress has really served good purpose if it wipes out so many of the things that make life worthwhile.

Evolution demonstrates the value of learning from mistakes; so perhaps we can evolve a subservient technology—one that follows man instead of leading him. The closing of Glen Canyon dam in our time was a major mistake to learn from, and our purpose here is to help the world remember these things lost.

There could be long and acrimonious debate over the accusation of mistake. Good men, who have plans for the Colorado River whereby "a natural menace becomes a natural resource," would argue tirelessly that the Colorado must be controlled, that its energy should be tapped and used to finance agricultural development in the arid west. But our point here is that for all their good intentions these men had too insular a notion of what man's relation to his environment should be, and it is tragic that their insularity was heeded. The natural Colorado—what is left of it—is a miracle, not a menace. The menace is more likely the notion that growth and progress are the same, and that the gross national product is the measure of the good life.

It is a well-documented fact that the Colorado River is being overdeveloped. A bookkeeping transaction could have served the ostensible purpose of Glen Canyon dam, which without that transaction emerges as a costly device to make sure water will flow downhill. What water this reservoir holds back for credit above the arbitrary division point of Lee's Ferry could be credited in Lake Mead much more economically and far less wastefully. The dam irrigates nothing. Instead, it evaporates an enormous quantity of water that could otherwise have irrigated land or supplied cities in an arid region that is short of water. To the extent reservoir storage adds to the already high mineral content of the water, the water's quality is diminished for all downstream use, including Mexico's. The transcendent purpose of the dam is to produce hydroelectric power, and the revenues incident thereto, which could finance irrigation of new and costly agriculture—as if there were no way to finance development of a region other than to sacrifice irretrievably its most important scenic assets—assets equaled nowhere else on earth.

Hoover, Parker, and Davis dams already exist and control the river adequately; they could probably continue to do so until Lake Mead is silted in completely, perhaps two hundred years from now. The Colorado–Big Thompson diversion project and developments like it which are already under way or planned will exploit the Colorado's waters upstream, where nearly half the flow has been allocated. Glen Canyon dam is a monument to man's lack of flexibility—to his having concluded that the only way to finance Reclamation is to sell the hydroelectric power produced by falling water of the streams he proposes to irrigate with. Revenue by other routes, including that from other sources of power which are already or will soon be less expensive to develop, was not politically attainable at the moment. This public failure—the inability to finance reasonable development of the West by means that financed it elsewhere—has cost all men, for all time, the miracle of an unspoiled Glen Canyon.

Other miracles will vanish by the same route unless we can learn from this mistake. The plans are well under way to eradicate the finest of those miracles left on the Colorado, as well as on other major rivers. A similar mistake was made early in the century at Hetch Hetchy in the Sierra Nevada, where a second Yosemite, now much needed for its natural beauty, was flooded to provide power for San Francisco. Alternative sources of water and power that could have saved Hetch Hetchy are still unused. Out of that mistake grew the National Park Act of 1916.[1] If the destruction of Glen Canyon leads indirectly to a diminishing of such forces of rapacity or can somehow correct the belief that man's only road to salvation is a paved one, then there will be some amelioration.

The alternatives that could have saved Glen Canyon are still unused. Fossil fuels, for one. The states of the Upper Basin of the Colorado contain a major part of the earth's coal reserves. The development of these resources is in the doldrums—and they are a much longer-lived source of energy than the short-lived reservoirs planned for the silty Colorado. Atomic and solar sources of energy will beyond doubt, generations before Lake Mead is silted in, make the destruction of Glen Canyon appear to have been the most naïve of choices in the search for electricity. Nothing our technology will have taught us, in this century or any other, will be able to put Glen Canyon back together again.

The Place No One Knew has a moral—which is why the Sierra Club publishes it—and the moral is simple: Progress need not deny to the people their inalienable right to be informed and to choose. In Glen Canyon the people never knew what the choices were. Next

---

[1]The National Park Act of 1916, also known as the "Organic Act," created the National Park Service. Brower, like other early environmentalists, believed that the parks had failed in their mission to "conserve the scenery and the natural and historic objects and the wild life therein."

time, in other stretches of the Colorado, on other rivers that are still free, and wherever there is wildness that can be part of our civilization instead of victim to it, the people need to know before a bureau's elite decide to wipe out what no men can replace. The Sierra Club has no better purpose than to try to let people know in time. In Glen Canyon we failed. There could hardly be a costlier peacetime mistake. With support from people who care, we hope in the years to come to help deter similar ravages of blind progress.

6

EDWARD ABBEY

Desert Solitaire

1968

In the late 1950s, Edward Abbey, a former philosophy student at the University of New Mexico, arrived at Arches National Monument in Utah to serve as a seasonal ranger. The journal Abbey kept while living in a trailer, later published as Desert Solitaire, *is a twentieth-century analogue to Thoreau's* Walden. *Nothing angered Abbey more than the economic development and commercial promotion of wilderness to make it more accessible to tourists in automobiles, what he called "industrial tourism." The sense of loss and defiance that first welled up in him at Arches never left him. He went on to write* The Monkey Wrench Gang *(1975), a novel about four people who plan to blow up Glen Canyon Dam on the Colorado River in order to save the Southwest from real-estate developers and government engineers. "Cactus Ed" Abbey was born in Home, Pennsylvania, in 1927. He died in 1989 and is rumored to be buried somewhere in the southwestern desert.*

Do not jump into your automobile next June and rush out to the Canyon country hoping to see some of that which I have attempted to evoke in these pages. In the first place you can't see *anything* from a

Edward Abbey, *Desert Solitaire: A Season in the Wilderness* (New York: Ballantine Books, 1968), xii, 51–52, 54–57.

car; you've got to get out of the goddamned contraption and walk, better yet crawl, on hands and knees, over the sandstone and through the
thornbush and cactus. When traces of blood begin to mark your trail
you'll see something, maybe. Probably not. In the second place most
of what I write about in this book is already gone or going under fast.
This is not a travel guide but an elegy. A memorial. You're holding a
tombstone in your hands. A bloody rock. Don't drop it on your foot—
throw it at something big and glassy. What do you have to lose? . . .

Where once a few adventurous people came on weekends to camp
for a night or two and enjoy a taste of the primitive and remote, you
will now find serpentine streams of baroque automobiles pouring in
and out, all through the spring and summer, in numbers that would
have seemed fantastic when I worked there: from 3,000 to 30,000 to
300,000 per year, the "visitation," as they call it, mounts ever upward.
The little campgrounds where I used to putter around reading three-
day-old newspapers full of lies and watermelon seeds have now been
consolidated into one master campground that looks, during the busy
season, like a suburban village: elaborate housetrailers of quilted aluminum crowd upon gigantic camper-trucks of Fiberglas and molded
plastic; through their windows you will see the blue glow of television
and hear the studio laughter of Los Angeles; knobby-kneed oldsters in
plaid Bermudas buzz up and down the quaintly curving asphalt road
on motorbikes; quarrels break out between campsite neighbors while
others gather around their burning charcoal briquettes (ground camp-
fires no longer permitted—not enough wood) to compare electric
toothbrushes. The Comfort Stations are there, too, all lit up with electricity, fully equipped inside, though the generator breaks down now
and then and the lights go out, or the sewage backs up in the plumbing system (drain fields were laid out in sand over a solid bed of sandstone), and the water supply sometimes fails, since the 3000-foot well
can only produce about 5gpm—not always enough to meet the
demand. Down at the beginning of the new road, at park headquarters, is the new entrance station and visitor center, where admission
fees are collected and where the rangers are going quietly nuts
answering the same three basic questions five hundred times a
day: (1) Where's the john? (2) How long's it take to see this place?
(3) Where's the Coke machine?

Progress has come at last to the Arches, after a million years of
neglect. Industrial Tourism has arrived. . . .

There may be some among the readers of this book . . . who believe
without question that any and all forms of construction and develop-

ment are intrinsic goods, in the national parks as well as anywhere else, who virtually identify quantity with quality and therefore assume that the greater the quantity of traffic, the higher the value received. There are some who frankly and boldly advocate the eradication of the last remnants of wilderness and the complete subjugation of nature to the requirements of—not man—but industry. This is a courageous view, admirable in its simplicity and power, and with the weight of all modern history behind it. It is also quite insane. I cannot attempt to deal with it here.

There will be other readers, I hope, who share my basic assumption that wilderness is a necessary part of civilization and that it is the primary responsibility of the national park system to preserve *intact* and *undiminished* what little still remains.

Most readers, while generally sympathetic to this latter point of view, will feel, as do the administrators of the National Park Service, that although wilderness is a fine thing, certain compromises and adjustments are necessary in order to meet the ever-expanding demand for outdoor recreation. It is precisely this question which I would like to examine now.

The Park Service, established by Congress in 1916, was directed not only to administer the parks but also to "provide for the enjoyment of same in such manner and by such means as will leave them unimpaired for the enjoyment of future generations." This appropriately ambiguous language, employed long before the onslaught of the automobile, has been understood in various and often opposing ways ever since. The Park Service, like any other big organization, includes factions and factions. The Developers, the dominant faction, place their emphasis on the words *"provide for the enjoyment."* The Preservers, a minority but also strong, emphasize the words *"leave them unimpaired."* It is apparent, then, that we cannot decide the question of development versus preservation by a simple referral to holy writ or an attempt to guess the intention of the founding fathers; we must make up our own minds and decide for ourselves what the national parks should be and what purpose they should serve.

The first issue that appears when we get into this matter, the most important issue and perhaps the only issue, is the one called *accessibility*. The Developers insist that the parks must be made fully accessible not only to people but also to their machines, that is, to automobiles, motorboats, etc. The Preservers argue, in principle at least, that wilderness and motors are incompatible and that the former can best be experienced, understood, and enjoyed when the machines are left behind where they belong—on the superhighways and in the parking lots, on the reservoirs and in the marinas.

What does accessibility mean? Is there any spot on earth that men have not proved accessible by the simplest means—feet and legs and heart? Even Mt. McKinley, even Everest, have been surmounted by men on foot. (Some of them, incidentally, rank amateurs, to the horror and indignation of the professional mountaineers.) The interior of the Grand Canyon, a fiercely hot and hostile abyss, is visited each summer by thousands and thousands of tourists of the most banal and unadventurous type, many of them on foot—self-propelled, so to speak—and the others on the backs of mules. Thousands climb each summer to the summit of Mt. Whitney, highest point in the forty-eight United States, while multitudes of others wander on foot or on horseback through the ranges of the Sierras, the Rockies, the Big Smokies, the Cascades and the mountains of New England. Still more hundreds and thousands float or paddle each year down the currents of the Salmon, the Snake, the Allagash, the Yampa, the Green, the Rio Grande, the Ozark, the St. Croix and those portions of the Colorado which have not yet been destroyed by the dam builders. And most significant, these hordes of nonmotorized tourists, hungry for a taste of the difficult, the original, the real, do not consist solely of people young and athletic but also of old folks, fat folks, pale-faced office clerks who don't know a rucksack from a haversack, and even children. The one thing they all have in common is the refusal to live always like sardines in a can—they are determined to get outside of their motorcars for at least a few weeks each year.

This being the case, why is the Park Service generally so anxious to accommodate that other crowd, the indolent millions born on wheels and suckled on gasoline, who expect and demand paved highways to lead them in comfort, ease and safety into every nook and corner of the national parks? For the answer to that we must consider the character of what I call Industrial Tourism and the quality of the mechanized tourists—the Wheelchair Explorers—who are at once the consumers, the raw material and the victims of Industrial Tourism.

Industrial Tourism is a big business. It means money. It includes the motel and restaurant owners, the gasoline retailers, the oil corporations, the road-building contractors, the heavy equipment manufacturers, the state and federal engineering agencies and the sovereign, all-powerful automotive industry. These various interests are well organized, command more wealth than most modern nations, and are represented in Congress with a strength far greater than is justified in any constitutional or democratic sense. (Modern politics is expensive—power follows money.) Through Congress the tourism industry can bring enormous pressure to bear upon such a slender reed in the executive branch as the poor old Park Service, a pressure which is also exerted on every other possible level—local, state, regional—and through advertising and the well-established habits of a wasteful nation.

When a new national park, national monument, national seashore, or whatever it may be called is set up, the various forces of Industrial Tourism, on all levels, immediately expect action—meaning specifically a road-building program. Where trails or primitive dirt roads already exist, the Industry expects—it hardly needs to ask—that these be developed into modern paved highways. On the local level, for example, the first thing that the superintendent of a new park can anticipate being asked, when he attends his first meeting of the area's Chamber of Commerce, is not "Will roads be built?" but rather "When does construction begin?" and "Why the delay?"

2

The End of Abundance

7

GARRETT HARDIN

The Tragedy of the Commons
1968

Environmentalists of the 1960s and 1970s believed that they had lived to see Thomas Malthus's principle of population (that population outpaces food supplies) become reality. They said that the world's resources, including its fresh water, arable land, oil reserves, forests, and open spaces, groaned under the stress of unprecedented human numbers and economic growth. In the years before Garrett Hardin published "The Tragedy of the Commons," the essay from which this excerpt is taken, humans left the earth's atmosphere for the first time, and they photographed a lonely blue planet (see page 3). The photograph offered a new image of terrestrial fragility and a new metaphor: Spaceship Earth. Hardin added another element: Competition to accumulate wealth results in resource depletion, because no one has a logical motive not to consume. The essay is a statement of environmental doom, driven by the same human nature that Malthus so feared.

A finite world can support only a finite population; therefore, population growth must eventually equal zero. (The case of perpetual wide fluctuations above and below zero is a trivial variant that need not be discussed.) When this condition is met, what will be the situation of

Garrett Hardin, "The Tragedy of the Commons," *Science* 162 (December 13, 1968): 1243–48.

mankind? Specifically, can Bentham's goal of "the greatest good for the greatest number" be realized?[1]

No—for two reasons, each sufficient by itself. The first is a theoretical one. It is not mathematically possible to maximize for two (or more) variables at the same time. . . .

The second reason springs directly from biological facts. To live, any organism must have a source of energy (for example, food). This energy is utilized for two purposes: mere maintenance and work. For man, maintenance of life requires about 1600 kilo-calories a day ("maintenance calories"). Anything that he does over and above merely staying alive will be defined as work, and is supported by "work calories" which he takes in. Work calories are used not only for what we call work in common speech; they are also required for all forms of enjoyment, from swimming and automobile racing to playing music and writing poetry. If our goal is to maximize population it is obvious what we must do: We must make the work calories per person approach as close to zero as possible. No gourmet meals, no vacations, no sports, no music, no literature, no art. . . . I think that everyone will grant, without argument or proof, that maximizing population does not maximize goods. Bentham's goal is impossible. . . .

The tragedy of the commons develops in this way. Picture a pasture open to all. It is to be expected that each herdsman will try to keep as many cattle as possible on the commons. Such an arrangement may work reasonably satisfactorily for centuries because tribal wars, poaching, and disease keep the numbers of both man and beast well below the carrying capacity of the land. Finally, however, comes the day of reckoning, that is, the day when the long-desired goal of social stability becomes a reality. At this point, the inherent logic of the commons remorselessly generates tragedy.

As a rational being, each herdsman seeks to maximize his gain. Explicitly or implicitly, more or less consciously, he asks, "What is the utility *to me* of adding one more animal to my herd?" This utility has one negative and one positive component.

1) The positive component is a function of the increment of one animal. Since the herdsman receives all the proceeds from the sale of the additional animal, the positive utility is nearly +1.

---

[1]English philosopher Jeremy Bentham (1748–1832) advocated utilitarianism—the idea that the rightness of an action depends entirely on its consequences and that human actions should strive to achieve "the greatest good for the greatest number."

2) The negative component is a function of the additional overgrazing created by one more animal. Since, however, the effects of overgrazing are shared by all the herdsmen, the negative utility for any particular decision-making herdsman is only a fraction of –1.

Adding together the component partial utilities, the rational herdsman concludes that the only sensible course for him to pursue is to add another animal to his herd. And another; and another. . . . But this is the conclusion reached by each and every rational herdsman sharing a commons. Therein is the tragedy. Each man is locked into a system that compels him to increase his herd without limit—in a world that is limited. Ruin is the destination toward which all men rush, each pursuing his own best interest in a society that believes in the freedom of the commons. Freedom in a commons brings ruin to all. . . .

In a reverse way, the tragedy of the commons reappears in problems of pollution. Here it is not a question of taking something out of the commons, but of putting something in—sewage, or chemical, radioactive, and heat wastes into water; noxious and dangerous fumes into the air; and distracting and unpleasant advertising signs into the line of sight. The calculations of utility are much the same as before. The rational man finds that his share of the cost of the wastes he discharges into the commons is less than the cost of purifying his wastes before releasing them. Since this is true for everyone, we are locked into a system of "fouling our own nest," so long as we behave only as independent, rational, free-enterprisers.

The tragedy of the commons as a food basket is averted by private property, or something formally like it. But the air and waters surrounding us cannot readily be fenced, and so the tragedy of the commons as a cesspool must be prevented by different means, by coercive laws or taxing devices that make it cheaper for the polluter to treat his pollutants than to discharge them untreated. We have not progressed as far with the solution of this problem as we have with the first. Indeed, our particular concept of private property, which deters us from exhausting the positive resources of the earth, favors pollution. The owner of a factory on the bank of a stream—whose property extends to the middle of the stream—often has difficulty seeing why it is not his natural right to muddy the waters flowing past his door. The law, always behind the times, requires elaborate stitching and fitting to adapt it to this newly perceived aspect of the commons.

The pollution problem is a consequence of population. It did not much matter how a lonely American frontiersman disposed of his waste. "Flowing water purifies itself every 10 miles," my grandfather used to say, and the myth was near enough to the truth when he was a boy, for there were not too many people. But as population became denser, the natural chemical and biological recycling processes became overloaded, calling for a redefinition of property rights.

Analysis of the pollution problem as a function of population density uncovers a not generally recognized principle of morality, namely: *the morality of an act is a function of the state of the system at the time it is performed.* Using the commons as a cesspool does not harm the general public under frontier conditions, because there is no public; the same behavior in a metropolis is unbearable. A hundred and fifty years ago a plainsman could kill an American bison, cut out only the tongue for his dinner, and discard the rest of the animal. He was not in any important sense being wasteful. Today, with only a few thousand bison left, we would be appalled at such behavior. . . .

Perhaps the simplest summary of this analysis of man's population problems is this: the commons, if justifiable at all, is justifiable only under conditions of low-population density. As the human population has increased, the commons has had to be abandoned in one aspect after another.

First we abandoned the commons in food gathering, enclosing farm land and restricting pastures and hunting and fishing areas. These restrictions are still not complete throughout the world.

Somewhat later we saw that the commons as a place for waste disposal would also have to be abandoned. Restrictions on the disposal of domestic sewage are widely accepted in the Western world; we are still struggling to close the commons to pollution by automobiles, factories, insecticide sprayers, fertilizing operations, and atomic energy installations.

In a still more embryonic state is our recognition of the evils of the commons in matters of pleasure. There is almost no restriction on the propagation of sound waves in the public medium. The shopping public is assaulted with mindless music, without its consent. Our government is paying out billions of dollars to create supersonic transport which will disturb 50,000 people for every one person who is whisked from coast to coast 3 hours faster. Advertisers muddy the airwaves of radio and television and pollute the view of travelers. We are a long way from outlawing the commons in matters of pleasure. Is this because our Puritan inheritance makes us view pleasure as something of a sin, and pain (that is, the pollution of advertising) as the sign of virtue?

Every new enclosure of the commons involves the infringement of somebody's personal liberty. Infringements made in the distant past are accepted because no contemporary complains of a loss. It is the newly proposed infringements that we vigorously oppose; cries of "rights" and "freedom" fill the air. But what does "freedom" mean? When men mutually agreed to pass laws against robbing, mankind became more free, not less so. Individuals locked into the logic of the commons are free only to bring on universal ruin; once they see the necessity of mutual coercion, they become free to pursue other goals. I believe it was Hegel who said, "Freedom is the recognition of necessity."

The most important aspect of necessity that we must now recognize, is the necessity of abandoning the commons in breeding. No technical solution can rescue us from the misery of overpopulation. Freedom to breed will bring ruin to all. At the moment, to avoid hard decisions many of us are tempted to propagandize for conscience and responsible parenthood. The temptation must be resisted, because an appeal to independently acting consciences selects for the disappearance of all conscience in the long run, and an increase in anxiety in the short.

The only way we can preserve and nurture other and more precious freedoms is by relinquishing the freedom to breed, and that very soon. "Freedom is the recognition of necessity"—and it is the role of education to reveal to all the necessity of abandoning the freedom to breed. Only so, can we put an end to this aspect of the tragedy of the commons.

8

PAUL EHRLICH

The Population Bomb

1968

The Population Bomb, by biologist Paul Ehrlich, became a bestseller after its publication in 1968 in spite of its call for immediate, drastic reductions in the world's population and its recommendation that the government add sterilizing chemicals to food and water to prevent people

Paul Ehrlich, *The Population Bomb* (New York: Ballantine Books, 1968), 131–36.

from reproducing. Since Malthus, advocates of population control have blamed poor people for producing children beyond their means to sustain them, although wealthy people consume far more resources per person than poor people do. Ehrlich insisted that the United States needed a population policy to stabilize its own consumption, but he also recommended that the government curtail food aid to developing countries that showed no signs of finding a balance between population and food supply. Ehrlich said that the poor should starve for being poor, and in this he was more like Malthus than any other Malthusian of the time.

A general answer to the question, "What needs to be done?" is simple. We must rapidly bring the world population under control, reducing the growth rate to zero or making it go negative. Conscious regulation of human numbers must be achieved. Simultaneously we must, at least temporarily, greatly increase our food production. This agricultural program should be carefully monitored to minimize deleterious effects on the environment and should include an effective program of ecosystem restoration. As these projects are carried out, an international policy research program must be initiated to set optimum population-environment goals for the world and to devise methods for reaching these goals. So the answer to the question is simple. Getting the job done, unfortunately, is going to be complex beyond belief—if indeed it can be done. What follows . . . are some ideas on how these goals *might* be reached and a brief assessment of our chances of reaching them.

The key to the whole business, in my opinion, is held by the United States. We are the most influential superpower; we are the richest nation in the world. At the same time we are also just one country on an ever-shrinking planet. It is obvious that we cannot exist unaffected by the fate of our fellows on the other end of the good ship Earth. If their end of the ship sinks, we shall at the very least have to put up with the spectacle of their drowning and listen to their screams. Communications satellites guarantee that we will be treated to the sights and sounds of mass starvation on the evening news, just as we now can see Viet Cong corpses being disposed of in living color and listen to the groans of our own wounded. We're unlikely, however, to get off with just our appetites spoiled and our consciences disturbed. We are going to be sitting on top of the only food surpluses available for distribution, and those surpluses will not be large. In addition, it is not unreasonable to expect our level of affluence to continue to increase over the next few years as the situation in the rest of the world grows ever more desperate. Can we guess what effect this growing disparity will have on our "shipmates" in the UDCs?[2] Will they starve gracefully, without rocking the boat? Or will they attempt to overwhelm us in order to get what they consider to be their fair share?

We, of course, cannot remain affluent and isolated. At the moment the United States uses well over half of all the raw materials consumed each year. Think of it. Less than 1/15th of the population of the world requires more than all the rest to maintain its inflated position. If present trends continue, in 20 years we will be much less than 1/15th of the population, and yet we may use some 80% of the resources consumed. Our affluence depends heavily on many different kinds of imports: ferroalloys (metals used to make various kinds of steel), tin, bauxite (aluminum ore), rubber, and so forth. Will other countries, many of them in the grip of starvation and anarchy, still happily supply these materials to a nation that cannot give them food? Even the technological optimists don't think we can free ourselves of the need for imports in the near future, so we're going to be up against it. But, then, at least our balance of payments should improve!

So, beside our own serious population problem at home, we are intimately involved in the world crisis. We are involved through our import-export situation. We are involved because of the possibilities of global ecological catastrophe, of global pestilence, and of global thermonuclear war. Also, we are involved because of the humanitarian feelings of most Americans.

We are going to face some extremely difficult but unavoidable decisions. By how much, and at what environmental risk, should we increase our food production in an attempt to feed the starving? How much should we reduce the grain-finishing of beef in order to have more food for export? How will we react when asked to balance the lives of a million Latin Americans against, say, a 30 cent per pound rise in the average price of beef? Will we be willing to slaughter our dogs and cats in order to divert pet food protein to the starving masses in Asia? If these choices are presented one at a time, out of context, I predict that our behavior will be "selfish." Men do not seem to be able to focus emotionally on distant or long-term events. Immediacy seems to be necessary to elicit "selfless" responses. Few Americans could sit in the same room with a child and watch it starve to death. But the death of several million children this year from starvation is a distant,

[2]Underdeveloped countries.

impersonal, hard-to-grasp event. You will note that I put quotes around "selfish" and "selfless." The words describe the behavior only out of context. The "selfless" actions necessary to aid the rest of the world and stabilize the population are our only hope for survival. The "selfish" ones work only toward our destruction. Ways must be found to bring home to all the American people the reality of the threat to their way of life—indeed to their very lives.

Obviously our first step must be to immediately establish and advertise drastic policies designed to bring our own population size under control. We must define a goal of a stable optimum population size for the United States and display our determination to move rapidly toward that goal. Such a move does two things at once. It improves our chances of obtaining the kind of country and society we all want, and it sets an example for the world. The second step is very important, as we also are going to have to adopt some very tough foreign policy positions relative to population control, and we must do it from a psychologically strong position. We will want to disarm one group of opponents at the outset: those who claim that we wish others to stop breeding while we go merrily ahead. We want our propaganda based on "do as we do"—not "do as we say."

So the first task is population control at home. How do we go about it? Many of my colleagues feel that some sort of compulsory birth regulation would be necessary to achieve such control. One plan often mentioned involves the addition of temporary sterilants to water supplies or staple food. Doses of the antidote would be carefully rationed by the government to produce the desired population size. Those of you who are appalled at such a suggestion can rest easy. The option isn't even open to us, thanks to the criminal inadequacy of biomedical research in this area. If the choice now is either such additives or catastrophe, we shall have catastrophe. It might be possible to develop such population control tools, although the task would not be simple. Either the additive would have to operate equally well and with minimum side effects against both sexes, or some way would have to be found to direct it only to one sex and shield the other. Feeding potent male hormones to the whole population might sterilize and defeminize the women, while the upset in the male population and society as a whole can be well imagined. In addition, care would have to be taken to see to it that the sterilizing substance did not reach livestock, either through water or garbage.

Technical problems aside, I suspect you'll agree with me that society would probably dissolve before sterilants were added to the water supply by the government. Just consider the fluoridation controversy! Some other way will have to be found. Perhaps the most workable system would be to reverse the government's present system of encouraging reproduction and replace it with a series of financial rewards and penalties designed to discourage reproduction.

9

DONELLA MEADOWS AND DENNIS MEADOWS

Limits to Growth

1972

Limits to Growth *is the purest statement of looming Malthusian catastrophe. Using a computer model developed at the Massachusetts Institute of Technology, researchers led by Donella Meadows entered rates and quantities of consumption, along with population data, to predict how long people could consume at their present rates before reaching a worldwide crisis. The team reached the conclusion that the world would run out of nonrenewable resources such as oil and farmland within a century and that, with resources depleted, a complete collapse of the economic system would follow. New forms of energy and the more efficient use of land would only put off the inevitable as population continued to rise and the food supply became the new limiting factor. Critics assailed the model as flawed, and many of its predictions have not yet come to pass, but its central question remains: How can finite matter and energy endure exponential growth?*

What will be needed to sustain world economic and population growth until, and perhaps even beyond, the year 2000? The list of necessary ingredients is long, but it can be divided roughly into two main categories.

Donella H. Meadows and Dennis Meadows, *Limits to Growth: A Report for the Club of Rome's Project on the Predicament of Mankind* (New York: Universe Books, 1972), 45–46, 50–54.

The first category includes the *physical* necessities that support all physiological and industrial activity—food, raw materials, fossil and nuclear fuels, and the ecological systems of the planet which absorb wastes and recycle important basic chemical substances. These ingredients are in principle tangible, countable items, such as arable land, fresh water, metals, forests, the oceans. In this chapter we will assess the world's stocks of these physical resources, since they are the ultimate determinants of the limits to growth on this earth.

The second category of necessary ingredients for growth consists of the *social* necessities. Even if the earth's physical systems are capable of supporting a much larger, more economically developed population, the actual growth of the economy and of the population will depend on such factors as peace and social stability, education and employment, and steady technological progress. These factors are much more difficult to assess or to predict. Neither this book nor our world model at this stage in its development can deal explicitly with these social factors, except insofar as our information about the quantity and distribution of physical supplies can indicate possible future social problems.

Food, resources, and a healthy environment are necessary but not sufficient conditions for growth. Even if they are abundant, growth may be stopped by social problems. Let us assume for the moment, however, that the best possible social conditions will prevail. How much growth will the physical system then support? The answer we obtain will give us some estimate of the upper limits to population and capital growth, but no guarantee that growth will actually proceed that far. . . .

[The] UN Food and Agriculture Organization (FAO) indicate[s] that in most of the developing countries basic caloric requirements, and particularly protein requirements, are not being supplied. Furthermore, although total world agricultural production is increasing, food production *per capita* in the nonindustrialized countries is barely holding constant at its present inadequate level. Do these rather dismal statistics mean that the limits of food production on the earth have already been reached?

The primary resource necessary for producing food is land. Recent studies indicate that there are, at most, about 3.2 billion hectares of land (7.86 billion acres) potentially suitable for agriculture on the earth. Approximately half of that land, the richest, most accessible half, is under cultivation today. The remaining land will require immense capital inputs to reach, clear, irrigate, or fertilize before it is ready to produce food. Recent costs of developing new land have ranged from $215 to $5,275 per hectare. Average cost for opening land in unsettled areas has been $1,150 per hectare. According to an FAO report, opening more land to cultivation is not economically feasible, even given the pressing need for food in the world today[.] . . .

If the world's people did decide to pay the high capital costs, to cultivate all possible arable land, and to produce as much food as possible, how many people could theoretically be fed? The lower curve in figure 10 shows the amount of land needed to feed the growing world population, assuming that the present world average of 0.4 hectares per person is sufficient. (To feed the entire world population at present US standards, 0.9 hectares per person would be required.) The upper curve in figure 10 shows the actual amount of arable land available over time. This line slopes downward because each additional person requires a certain amount of land (0.08 hectares per person assumed here) for housing, roads, waste disposal, power lines, and other uses that essentially "pave" arable land and make it unusable for food production. Land loss through erosion is not shown here, but it is by no means negligible. Figure 10 shows that, even with the optimistic assumption that all possible land is utilized, there will still be a desperate land shortage before the year 2000 if per capita land requirements and population growth rates remain as they are today.

[The figure on page 65] also illustrates some very important general facts about exponential growth within a limited space. First, it shows how one can move within a very few years from a situation of great abundance to one of great scarcity. There has been an overwhelming excess of potentially arable land for all of history, and now, within 30 years (or about one population doubling time), there may be a sudden and serious shortage. . . .

Of course, society will not be suddenly surprised by the "crisis point" at which the amount of land needed becomes greater than that available. Symptoms of the crisis will begin to appear long before the crisis point is reached. Food prices will rise so high that some people will starve; others will be forced to decrease the effective amount of land they use and shift to lower quality diets. These symptoms are already apparent in many parts of the world. Although only half the land shown in [the figure] is now under cultivation, perhaps 10 to 20 million deaths each year can be attributed directly or indirectly to malnutrition.

There is no question that many of these deaths are due to the world's social limitations rather than its physical ones. Yet there is

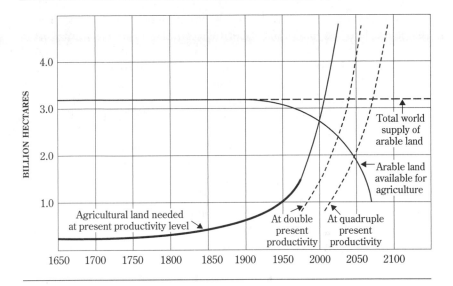

Arable Land

Total world supply of arable land is about 3.2 billion hectares. About 0.4 hectares per person of arable land are needed at present productivity. The curve of land needed thus reflects the population growth curve. The light line after 1970 shows the projected need for land, assuming that world population continues to grow at its present rate. Arable land available decreases because arable land is removed for urban-industrial use as population grows. The dotted curves show land needed if present productivity is doubled or quadrupled.

clearly a link between these two kinds of limitations in the food-producing system. If good fertile land were still easily reached and brought under cultivation, there would be no economic barrier to feeding the hungry, and no difficult social choices to make. The best half of the world's potentially arable land is already cultivated, however, and opening new land is already so costly that society has judged it "uneconomic." This is a social problem exacerbated by a physical limitation.

Even if society did decide to pay the necessary costs to gain new land or to increase productivity of the land already cultivated, figure 10 shows how quickly rising population would bring about another "crisis point." And each successive crisis point will cost more to overcome. Each doubling of yield from the land will be more expensive than the last one. We might call this phenomenon the law of increasing costs. The best and most sobering example of that law comes from an assessment of the cost of past agricultural gains. To achieve a 34 percent increase in world food production from 1951 to 1966, agriculturalists increased yearly expenditures on tractors by 63 percent, annual investment in nitrate fertilizers by 146 percent, and annual use of pesticides by 300 percent. The next 34 percent increase will require even greater inputs of capital and resources.

How many people can be fed on this earth? There is, of course, no simple answer to this question. The answer depends on the choices society makes among various available alternatives. There is a direct trade-off between producing more food and producing other goods and services needed or desired by mankind. The demand for these other goods and services is also increasing as population grows, and therefore the trade-off becomes continuously more apparent and more difficult to resolve. Even if the choice were consistently to produce food as the first priority, however, continued population growth and the law of increasing costs could rapidly drive the system to the point where all available resources were devoted to producing food, leaving no further possibility of expansion.

In this section we have discussed only one possible limit to food production—arable land. There are other possible limits, but space does not permit us to discuss them in detail here. The most obvious one, second in importance only to land, is the availability of fresh water. There is an upper limit to the fresh water runoff from the land areas of the earth each year, and there is also an exponentially increasing demand for that water. We could draw a graph exactly analogous to figure 10 to show the approach of the increasing demand curve for water to the constant average supply. In some areas of the world, this limit will be reached long before the land limit becomes apparent.

10

LESTER BROWN

Outgrowing the Earth

2004

Founded in 1974 by Lester Brown, Worldwatch Institute was the first research organization devoted to studying the global environment. Brown served in the U.S. Department of Agriculture's Foreign Agricultural Service, and the balance between food and population became the core concern of Worldwatch. Its annual State of the World report keeps track of this and other global trends, such as falling water tables and rising temperatures, both of which Brown believes will affect the ability of people to feed themselves in the century to come. In this excerpt from Outgrowing the Earth, *Brown argues that our food supply will soon become inadequate and, perhaps, a national security issue because of rapid population growth, the inability of farmers to keep up with demands for grain, and the excessive demands the world economy is making on the environment. Brown is significant because he is among the few "new Malthusians" still writing.*

As the economy grows, its demands are outgrowing the earth, exceeding many of the planet's natural capacities. While the world economy multiplied sevenfold in just 50 years, the earth's natural life-support systems remained essentially the same. Water use tripled, but the capacity of the hydrological system to produce fresh water through evaporation changed little. The demand for seafood increased fivefold, but the sustainable yield of oceanic fisheries was unchanged. Fossil fuel burning raised carbon dioxide (CO_2) emissions fourfold, but the capacity of nature to absorb CO_2 changed little, leading to a buildup of CO_2 in the atmosphere and a rise in the earth's temperature. As human demands surpass the earth's natural capacities, expanding food production becomes more difficult.

Lester Brown, *Outgrowing the Earth: The Food Security Challenge in an Age of Falling Water Tables and Rising Temperatures* (New York: W. W. Norton, 2004), 3–9, 193–94.

Losing Agricultural Momentum

Environmentalists have been saying for years that if the environmental trends of recent decades continued the world would one day be in trouble. What was not clear was what form the trouble would take and when it would occur. It now seems likely to take the form of tightening food supplies, and within the next few years. Indeed, China's forays into the world market in early 2004 to buy 8 million tons of wheat could mark the beginning of the global shift from an era of grain surpluses to one of grain scarcity.

World grain production is a basic indicator of dietary adequacy at the individual level and of overall food security at the global level. After nearly tripling from 1950 to 1996, the grain harvest stayed flat for seven years in a row, through 2003, showing no increase at all. And in each of the last four of those years, production fell short of consumption. The shortfalls of nearly 100 million tons in 2002 and again in 2003 were the largest on record.

With consumption exceeding production for four years, world grain stocks dropped to the lowest level in 30 years. The last time stocks were this low, in 1972–74, wheat and rice prices doubled. Importing countries competed vigorously for inadequate supplies. A politics of scarcity emerged—with some countries, such as the United States, restricting exports.

In 2004 a combination of stronger grain prices at planting time and the best weather in a decade yielded a substantially larger harvest for the first time in eight years. Yet even with a harvest that was up 124 million tons from that in 2003, the world still consumed all the grain it produced, leaving none to rebuild stocks. If stocks cannot be rebuilt in a year of exceptional weather, when can they?

From 1950 to 1984 world grain production expanded faster than population, raising the grain produced per person from 250 kilograms to the historical peak of 339 kilograms, an increase of 34 percent. This positive development initially reflected recovery from the disruption of World War II, and then later solid technological advances. The rising tide of food production lifted all ships, largely eradicating hunger in some countries and substantially reducing it in many others.

Since 1984, however, grain harvest growth has fallen behind that of population, dropping the amount of grain produced per person to 308 kilograms in 2004, down 9 percent from its historic high point. Fortunately, part of the global decline was offset by the increasing efficiency with which feedgrains are converted into animal protein, thanks to the growing use of soybean meal as a protein supplement. Accordingly, the deterioration in nutrition has not been as great as the bare numbers would suggest.

The one region where the decline in grain produced per person is unusually steep and where it is taking a heavy human toll is Africa. In addition to the nutrient depletion of soils and the steady shrinkage in grainland per person from population growth in recent decades, Africa must now contend with the loss of adults to AIDS, which is depleting the rural work force and undermining agriculture. From 1960 through 1981, grain production per person in sub-Saharan Africa ranged between 140 and 160 kilograms per person. Then from 1980 through 2001 it fluctuated largely between 120 and 140 kilograms. And in two of the last three years, it has been below 120 kilograms—dropping to a level that leaves millions of Africans on the edge of starvation.

Several long-standing environmental trends are contributing to the global loss of agricultural momentum. Among these are the cumulative effects of soil erosion on land productivity, the loss of cropland to desertification, and the accelerating conversion of cropland to nonfarm uses. All are taking a toll, although their relative roles vary among countries.

Now two newer environmental trends—falling water tables and rising temperatures—are slowing the growth in world food production.... In addition, farmers are faced with a shrinking backlog of unused technology. The high-yielding varieties of wheat, rice, and corn that were developed a generation or so ago are now widely used in industrial and developing countries alike. They doubled and tripled yields, but there have not been any dramatic advances in the genetic yield potential of grains since then.

The use of fertilizer, which removed nutrient constraints and helped the new high-yielding varieties realize their full genetic potential during the last half-century, has now plateaued or even declined slightly in key food-producing countries. Among these are the United States, countries in Western Europe, Japan, and now possibly China as well. Meanwhile, the rapid growth in irrigation that characterized much of the last half-century has also slowed. Indeed, in some countries the irrigated area is shrinking.

The bottom line is that it is now more difficult for farmers to keep up with the growing demand for grain. The rise in world grainland productivity, which averaged over 2 percent a year from 1950 to 1990, fell to scarcely 1 percent a year from 1990 to 2000. This will likely drop further in the years immediately ahead.

If the rise in land productivity continues to slow and if population continues to grow by 70 million or more per year, governments may begin to define national security in terms of food shortages, rising food prices, and the emerging politics of scarcity. Food insecurity may soon eclipse terrorism as the overriding concern of national governments.

Growth: The Environmental Fallout

The world economy, as now structured, is making excessive demands on the earth. Evidence of this can be seen in collapsing fisheries, shrinking forests, expanding deserts, rising CO_2 levels, eroding soils, rising temperatures, falling water tables, melting glaciers, deteriorating grasslands, rising seas, rivers that are running dry, and disappearing species.

Nearly all these environmentally destructive trends adversely affect the world food prospect. For example, even a modest rise of 1 degree Fahrenheit in temperature in mountainous regions can substantially increase rainfall and decrease snowfall. The result is more flooding during the rainy season and less snowmelt to feed rivers during the dry season, when farmers need irrigation water.

Or consider the collapse of fisheries and the associated leveling off of the oceanic fish catch. During the last half-century the fivefold growth in the world fish catch that satisfied much of the growing demand for animal protein pushed oceanic fisheries to their limits and beyond. Now, in this new century, we cannot expect any growth at all in the catch. All future growth in animal protein supplies can only come from the land, putting even more pressure on the earth's land and water resources.

Farmers have long had to cope with the cumulative effects of soil erosion on land productivity, the loss of cropland to nonfarm uses, and the encroachment of deserts on cropland. Now they are also being battered by higher temperatures and crop-scorching heat waves. Likewise, farmers who once had assured supplies of irrigation water are now forced to abandon irrigation as aquifers are depleted and wells go dry. Collectively this array of environmental trends is making it even more difficult for farmers to feed adequately the 70 million people added to our ranks each year.

Until recently, the economic effects of environmental trends, such as overfishing, overpumping, and overplowing, were largely local. Among the many examples are the collapse of the cod fishery off

Newfoundland from overfishing that cost Canada 40,000 jobs, the halving of Saudi Arabia's wheat harvest as a result of aquifer depletion, and the shrinking grain harvest of Kazakhstan as wind erosion claimed half of its cropland.

Now, if world food supplies tighten, we may see the first global economic effect of environmentally destructive trends. Rising food prices could be the first economic indicator to signal serious trouble in the deteriorating relationship between the global economy and the earth's ecosystem. The short-lived 20-percent rise in world grain prices in early 2004 may turn out to be a warning tremor before the quake. . . .

In a world that is increasingly integrated economically, food security is now a global issue. In an integrated world grain market, everyone is affected by the same price shifts. A doubling of grain prices, which is a distinct possibility if we cannot accelerate the growth in grain production, could impoverish more people and destabilize more governments than any event in history. Our future depends on working together to avoid a destabilizing jump in world food prices. Everyone has a stake in stabilizing the agricultural resource base. Everyone has a stake in securing future food supplies. We all have a responsibility to work for the policies—whether in agriculture, energy, population, water use, cropland protection, or soil conservation—that will help ensure future world food security.

The complexity of the challenges the world is facing is matched by the enormity of the effort required to reverse the trends that are undermining future food security. Halting the advancing deserts in China, arresting the fall in water tables in India, and reversing the rise in carbon emissions in the United States are each essential to future world food security. Each will require a strong, new initiative—one that demands a wartime sense of urgency and leadership.

We have inherited the mindset, policies, and fiscal priorities from an era of food security that no longer exists. The policies that once provided food security will no longer suffice in a world where we are pressing against the sustainable yields of oceanic fisheries and underground aquifers and the limits of nature to fix carbon dioxide. Unless we recognize the nature of the era we are entering and adopt new policies and priorities that recognize the earth's natural limits, world food security could begin to deteriorate. If it does, food security could quickly eclipse terrorism as the overriding concern of governments.

3

Ecology and Society

11

ALDO LEOPOLD

Thinking like a Mountain

1949

Ecology made it possible to envision humans as members of biotic communities, a term invented by Aldo Leopold that emphasizes the obligations humans have to plants and animals. Whenever wildlife managers, like Leopold himself, eliminated predators in a region, the results were not what they predicted. In this essay, Leopold refers to an explosive increase in the deer population of the Kaibab Plateau, near the Grand Canyon, in which deer were said to triple, even quadruple, after the removal of wolves during the 1920s. It may not have happened as Leopold thought (no one conducted a comprehensive survey, and ecologists doubt that the deer reached 100,000), but news of the event impressed him deeply. "Thinking like a Mountain" describes the central epiphany of his career and a defining moment in environmental thought. Leopold's empathic response to the mountain suggested that human influence over the earth had moral, if not technological, limits.

A deep chesty bawl echoes from rimrock to rimrock, rolls down the mountain, and fades into the far blackness of the night. It is an outburst of wild defiant sorrow, and of contempt for all the adversities of the world.

Aldo Leopold, *A Sand County Almanac* (New York: Oxford University Press, 1949), 129–33, 203–5.

Every living thing (and perhaps many a dead one as well) pays heed to that call. To the deer it is a reminder of the way of all flesh, to the pine a forecast of midnight scuffles and of blood upon the snow, to the coyote a promise of gleanings to come, to the cowman a threat of red ink at the bank, to the hunter a challenge of fang against bullet. Yet behind these obvious and immediate hopes and fears there lies a deeper meaning, known only to the mountain itself. Only the mountain has lived long enough to listen objectively to the howl of a wolf.

Those unable to decipher the hidden meaning know nevertheless that it is there, for it is felt in all wolf country, and distinguishes that country from all other land. It tingles in the spine of all who hear wolves by night, or who scan their tracks by day. Even without sight or sound of wolf, it is implicit in a hundred small events: the midnight whinny of a pack horse, the rattle of rolling rocks, the bound of a fleeing deer, the way shadows lie under the spruces. Only the ineducable tyro can fail to sense the presence or absence of wolves, or the fact that mountains have a secret opinion about them.

My own conviction on this score dates from the day I saw a wolf die. We were eating lunch on a high rimrock, at the foot of which a turbulent river elbowed its way. We saw what we thought was a doe fording the torrent, her breast awash in white water. When she climbed the bank toward us and shook out her tail, we realized our error: it was a wolf. A half-dozen others, evidently grown pups, sprang from the willows and all joined in a welcoming mêlée of wagging tails and playful maulings. What was literally a pile of wolves writhed and tumbled in the center of an open flat at the foot of our rimrock.

In those days we had never heard of passing up a chance to kill a wolf. In a second we were pumping lead into the pack, but with more excitement than accuracy: how to aim a steep downhill shot is always confusing. When our rifles were empty, the old wolf was down, and a pup was dragging a leg into impassable slide-rocks.

We reached the old wolf in time to watch a fierce green fire dying in her eyes. I realized then, and have known ever since, that there was something new to me in those eyes—something known only to her and to the mountain. I was young then, and full of trigger-itch; I thought that because fewer wolves meant more deer, that no wolves would mean hunters' paradise. But after seeing the green fire die, I sensed that neither the wolf nor the mountain agreed with such a view.

Since then I have lived to see state after state extirpate its wolves. I have watched the face of many a newly wolfless mountain, and seen the south-facing slopes wrinkle with a maze of new deer trails. I have seen every edible bush and seedling browsed, first to anaemic desuetude, and then to death. I have seen every edible tree defoliated to the height of a saddlehorn. Such a mountain looks as if someone had given God a new pruning shears, and forbidden Him all other exercise. In the end the starved bones of the hoped-for deer herd, dead of its own too-much, bleach with the bones of the dead sage, or molder under the high-lined junipers.

I now suspect that just as a deer herd lives in mortal fear of its wolves, so does a mountain live in mortal fear of its deer. And perhaps with better cause, for while a buck pulled down by wolves can be replaced in two or three years, a range pulled down by too many deer may fail of replacement in as many decades.

So also with cows. The cowman who cleans his range of wolves does not realize that he is taking over the wolf's job of trimming the herd to fit the range. He has not learned to think like a mountain. Hence we have dustbowls, and rivers washing the future into the sea.

We all strive for safety, prosperity, comfort, long life, and dullness. The deer strives with his supple legs, the cowman with trap and poison, the statesman with pen, the most of us with machines, votes, and dollars, but it all comes to the same thing: peace in our time. A measure of success in this is all well enough, and perhaps is a requisite to objective thinking, but too much safety seems to yield only danger in the long run. Perhaps this is behind Thoreau's dictum: In wildness is the salvation of the world. Perhaps this is the hidden meaning in the howl of the wolf, long known among mountains, but seldom perceived among men. . . .

The Community Concept

All ethics so far evolved rest upon a single premise: that the individual is a member of a community of interdependent parts. His instincts prompt him to compete for his place in that community, but his ethics prompt him also to co-operate (perhaps in order that there may be a place to compete for).

The land ethic simply enlarges the boundaries of the community to include soils, waters, plants, and animals, or collectively: the land.

This sounds simple: do we not already sing our love for and obligation to the land of the free and the home of the brave? Yes, but just what and whom do we love? Certainly not the soil, which we are sending helter-skelter downriver. Certainly not the waters, which we assume have no function except to turn turbines, float barges, and carry off sewage. Certainly not the plants, of which we exterminate whole communities without batting an eye. Certainly not the animals, of which we have already extirpated many of the largest and most beautiful species. A land ethic of course cannot prevent the alteration, management, and use of these "resources," but it does affirm their right to continued existence, and, at least in spots, their continued existence in a natural state.

In short, a land ethic changes the role of *Homo sapiens* from conqueror of the land-community to plain member and citizen of it. It implies respect for his fellow-members, and also respect for the community as such.

In human history, we have learned (I hope) that the conqueror role is eventually self-defeating. Why? Because it is implicit in such a role that the conqueror knows, *ex cathedra*, just what makes the community clock tick, and just what and who is valuable, and what and who is worthless, in community life. It always turns out that he knows neither, and this is why his conquests eventually defeat themselves.

In the biotic community, a parallel situation exists. Abraham knew exactly what the land was for: it was to drip milk and honey into Abraham's mouth.[1] At the present moment, the assurance with which we regard this assumption is inverse to the degree of our education.

The ordinary citizen today assumes that science knows what makes the community clock tick; the scientist is equally sure that he does not. He knows that the biotic mechanism is so complex that its workings may never be fully understood.

That man is, in fact, only a member of a biotic team is shown by an ecological interpretation of history. Many historical events, hitherto explained solely in terms of human enterprise, were actually biotic interactions between people and land. The characteristics of the land determined the facts quite as potently as the characteristics of the men who lived on it.

---

[1] In the Torah, Abraham was the man chosen by God to establish monotheism. In Deuteronomy 6:3 and 26:9, Moses refers to the land of Israel as "flowing with milk and honey."

12

RACHEL CARSON

Silent Spring

1962

Silent Spring is the single most important book in the birth of environmentalism because of the vast popular audience it reached and because of its unprecedented message. Its publication was one of the events, along with Earth Day 1970, that first suggested that environmentalism might become a movement with a broad constituency. Carson confronted two forces considered to have delivered the triumphant victory of World War II and the rising American standard of living: science and business. She revealed that neither understood how DDT affected soils, animals, beneficial insects such as bees, or humans. In this excerpt, Carson follows the delicate and insidious path taken by chemical pesticides through the food chain and points out that they represent "a hazard we ourselves have introduced into our world as our modern way of life has evolved" (187). Carson died of cancer in 1964. Congress banned the use of DDT in 1972.

The history of life on earth has been a history of interaction between living things and their surroundings. To a large extent, the physical form and the habits of the earth's vegetation and its animal life have been molded by the environment. Considering the whole span of earthly time, the opposite effect, in which life actually modifies its surroundings, has been relatively slight. Only within the moment of time represented by the present century has one species—man—acquired significant power to alter the nature of his world.

During the past quarter century this power has not only increased to one of disturbing magnitude but it has changed in character. The most alarming of all man's assaults upon the environment is the contamination of air, earth, rivers, and sea with dangerous and even lethal materials. This pollution is for the most part irrecoverable; the chain of evil it initiates not only in the world that must support life but in liv-

Rachel Carson, *Silent Spring* (New York: Houghton Mifflin, 1962), 5–13.

ing tissues is for the most part irreversible. In this now universal contamination of the environment, chemicals are the sinister and little-recognized partners of radiation in changing the very nature of the world—the very nature of its life. Strontium 90, released through nuclear explosions into the air, comes to earth in rain or drifts down as fallout, lodges in soil, enters into the grass or corn or wheat grown there, and in time takes up its abode in the bones of a human being, there to remain until his death. Similarly, chemicals sprayed on croplands or forests or gardens lie long in soil, entering into living organisms, passing from one to another in a chain of poisoning and death. Or they pass mysteriously by underground streams until they emerge and, through the alchemy of air and sunlight, combine into new forms that kill vegetation, sicken cattle, and work unknown harm on those who drink from once pure wells. As Albert Schweitzer has said, "Man can hardly even recognize the devils of his own creation."

It took hundreds of millions of years to produce the life that now inhabits the earth—eons of time in which that developing and evolving and diversifying life reached a state of adjustment and balance with its surroundings. The environment, rigorously shaping and directing the life it supported, contained elements that were hostile as well as supporting. Certain rocks gave out dangerous radiation; even within the light of the sun, from which all life draws its energy, there were short-wave radiations with power to injure. Given time—time not in years but in millennia—life adjusts, and a balance has been reached. For time is the essential ingredient; but in the modern world there is no time.

The rapidity of change and the speed with which new situations are created follow the impetuous and heedless pace of man rather than the deliberate pace of nature. Radiation is no longer merely the background radiation of rocks, the bombardment of cosmic rays, the ultra-violet of the sun that have existed before there was any life on earth; radiation is now the unnatural creation of man's tampering with the atom. The chemicals to which life is asked to make its adjustment are no longer merely the calcium and silica and copper and all the rest of the minerals washed out of the rocks and carried in rivers to the sea; they are the synthetic creations of man's inventive mind, brewed in his laboratories, and having no counterparts in nature.

To adjust to these chemicals would require time on the scale that is nature's; it would require not merely the years of a man's life but the life of generations. And even this, were it by some miracle possible, would be futile, for the new chemicals come from our laboratories in an endless stream; almost five hundred annually find their way into actual use in the United States alone. The figure is staggering and its implications are not easily grasped—500 new chemicals to which the bodies of men and animals are required somehow to adapt each year, chemicals totally outside the limits of biologic experience.

Among them are many that are used in man's war against nature. Since the mid-1940's over 200 basic chemicals have been created for use in killing insects, weeds, rodents, and other organisms described in the modern vernacular as "pests"; and they are sold under several thousand different brand names.

These sprays, dusts, and aerosols are now applied almost universally to farms, gardens, forests, and homes—nonselective chemicals that have the power to kill every insect, the "good" and the "bad," to still the song of birds and the leaping of fish in the streams, to coat the leaves with a deadly film, and to linger on in soil—all this though the intended target may be only a few weeds or insects. Can anyone believe it is possible to lay down such a barrage of poisons on the surface of the earth without making it unfit for all life? They should not be called "insecticides," but "biocides."

The whole process of spraying seems caught up in an endless spiral. Since DDT was released for civilian use, a process of escalation has been going on in which ever more toxic materials must be found. This has happened because insects, in a triumphant vindication of Darwin's principle of the survival of the fittest, have evolved super races immune to the particular insecticide used, hence a deadlier one has always to be developed—and then a deadlier one than that. It has happened also because . . . destructive insects often undergo a "flare-back," or resurgence, after spraying, in numbers greater than before. Thus the chemical war is never won, and all life is caught in its violent crossfire.

Along with the possibility of the extinction of mankind by nuclear war, the central problem of our age has therefore become the contamination of man's total environment with such substances of incredible potential for harm—substances that accumulate in the tissues of plants and animals and even penetrate the germ cells to shatter or alter the very material of heredity upon which the shape of the future depends.

Some would-be architects of our future look toward a time when it will be possible to alter the human germ plasm by design. But we may easily be doing so now by inadvertence, for many chemicals, like radiation, bring about gene mutations. It is ironic to think that man might determine his own future by something so seemingly trivial as the choice of an insect spray.

All this has been risked—for what? Future historians may well be amazed by our distorted sense of proportion. How could intelligent beings seek to control a few unwanted species by a method that contaminated the entire environment and brought the threat of disease and death even to their own kind? Yet this is precisely what we have done. We have done it, moreover, for reasons that collapse the moment we examine them. We are told that the enormous and expanding use of pesticides is necessary to maintain farm production. Yet is our real problem not one of *overproduction*? Our farms, despite measures to remove acreages from production and to pay farmers *not* to produce, have yielded such a staggering excess of crops that the American taxpayer in 1962 is paying out more than one billion dollars a year as the total carrying cost of the surplus-food storage program. And is the situation helped when one branch of the Agriculture Department tries to reduce production while another states, as it did in 1958, "It is believed generally that reduction of crop acreages under provisions of the Soil Bank will stimulate interest in use of chemicals to obtain maximum production on the land retained in crops."

All this is not to say there is no insect problem and no need of control. I am saying, rather, that control must be geared to realities, not to mythical situations, and that the methods employed must be such that they do not destroy us along with the insects.

The problem whose attempted solution has brought such a train of disaster in its wake is an accompaniment of our modern way of life. Long before the age of man, insects inhabited the earth—a group of extraordinarily varied and adaptable beings. Over the course of time since man's advent, a small percentage of the more than half a million species of insects have come into conflict with human welfare in two principal ways: as competitors for the food supply and as carriers of human disease.

Disease-carrying insects become important where human beings are crowded together, especially under conditions where sanitation is poor, as in time of natural disaster or war or in situations of extreme poverty and deprivation. Then control of some sort becomes necessary. It is a sobering fact, however, as we shall presently see, that the method of massive chemical control has had only limited success, and also threatens to worsen the very conditions it is intended to curb.

Under primitive agricultural conditions the farmer had few insect problems. These arose with the intensification of agriculture—the devotion of immense acreages to a single crop. Such a system set the stage for explosive increases in specific insect populations. Single-crop farming does not take advantage of the principles by which nature works; it is agriculture as an engineer might conceive it to be. Nature has introduced great variety into the landscape, but man has displayed a passion for simplifying it. Thus he undoes the built-in checks and balances by which nature holds the species within bounds. One important natural check is a limit on the amount of suitable habitat for each species. Obviously then, an insect that lives on wheat can build up its population to much higher levels on a farm devoted to wheat than on one in which wheat is intermingled with other crops to which the insect is not adapted.

The same thing happens in other situations. A generation or more ago, the towns of large areas of the United States lined their streets with the noble elm tree. Now the beauty they hopefully created is threatened with complete destruction as disease sweeps through the elms, carried by a beetle that would have only limited chance to build up large populations and to spread from tree to tree if the elms were only occasional trees in a richly diversified planting.

Another factor in the modern insect problem is one that must be viewed against a background of geologic and human history: the spreading of thousands of different kinds of organisms from their native homes to invade new territories. This worldwide migration has been studied and graphically described by the British ecologist Charles Elton in his recent book *The Ecology of Invasions*. During the Cretaceous Period, some hundred million years ago, flooding seas cut many land bridges between continents and living things found themselves confined in what Elton calls "colossal separate nature reserves." There, isolated from others of their kind, they developed many new species. When some of the land masses were joined again, about 15 million years ago, these species began to move out into new territories—a movement that is not only still in progress but is now receiving considerable assistance from man.

The importation of plants is the primary agent in the modern spread of species, for animals have almost invariably gone along with the plants, quarantine being a comparatively recent and not completely effective innovation. The United States Office of Plant Introduction alone has introduced almost 200,000 species and varieties of plants from all over the world. Nearly half of the 180 or so major insect enemies of plants in the United States are accidental imports from abroad, and most of them have come as hitchhikers on plants.

In new territory, out of reach of the restraining hand of the natural enemies that kept down its numbers in its native land, an invading plant or animal is able to become enormously abundant. Thus it is no accident that our most troublesome insects are introduced species.

These invasions, both the naturally occurring and those dependent on human assistance, are likely to continue indefinitely. Quarantine and massive chemical campaigns are only extremely expensive ways of buying time. We are faced, according to Dr. Elton, "with a life-and-death need not just to find new technological means of suppressing this plant or that animal"; instead we need the basic knowledge of animal populations and their relations to their surroundings that will "promote an even balance and damp down the explosive power of outbreaks and new invasions."

Much of the necessary knowledge is now available but we do not use it. We train ecologists in our universities and even employ them in our governmental agencies but we seldom take their advice. We allow the chemical death rain to fall as though there were no alternative, whereas in fact there are many, and our ingenuity could soon discover many more if given opportunity.

Have we fallen into a mesmerized state that makes us accept as inevitable that which is inferior or detrimental, as though having lost the will or the vision to demand that which is good? Such thinking, in the words of the ecologist Paul Shepard, "idealizes life with only its head out of water, inches above the limits of toleration of the corruption of its own environment[.] ... Why should we tolerate a diet of weak poisons, a home in insipid surroundings, a circle of acquaintances who are not quite our enemies, the noise of motors with just enough relief to prevent insanity? Who would want to live in a world which is just not quite fatal?"

Yet such a world is pressed upon us. The crusade to create a chemically sterile, insect-free world seems to have engendered a fanatic zeal on the part of many specialists and most of the so-called control agencies. On every hand there is evidence that those engaged in spraying operations exercise a ruthless power. "The regulatory entomologists ... function as prosecutor, judge and jury, tax assessor and collector and sheriff to enforce their own orders," said Connecticut entomologist Neely Turner. The most flagrant abuses go unchecked in both state and federal agencies.

It is not my contention that chemical insecticides must never be used. I do contend that we have put poisonous and biologically potent chemicals indiscriminately into the hands of persons largely or wholly ignorant of their potentials for harm. We have subjected enormous numbers of people to contact with these poisons, without their consent and often without their knowledge. If the Bill of Rights contains no guarantee that a citizen shall be secure against lethal poisons distributed either by private individuals or by public officials, it is surely only because our forefathers, despite their considerable wisdom and foresight, could conceive of no such problem.

I contend, furthermore, that we have allowed these chemicals to be used with little or no advance investigation of their effect on soil, water, wildlife, and man himself. Future generations are unlikely to condone our lack of prudent concern for the integrity of the natural world that supports all life.

There is still very limited awareness of the nature of the threat. This is an era of specialists, each of whom sees his own problem and is unaware of or intolerant of the larger frame into which it fits. It is also an era dominated by industry, in which the right to make a dollar at whatever cost is seldom challenged. When the public protests, confronted with some obvious evidence of damaging results of pesticide applications, it is fed little tranquilizing pills of half truth. We urgently need an end to these false assurances, to the sugar coating of unpalatable facts. It is the public that is being asked to assume the risks that the insect controllers calculate. The public must decide whether it wishes to continue on the present road, and it can do so only when in full possession of the facts. In the words of Jean Rostand, "The obligation to endure gives us the right to know."

13

BARRY COMMONER

The Closing Circle

1971

Ecosystems never deplete their resources and never produce waste, and this has been their attraction for social thinkers who began to apply their principles to the ways that humans organize production and consumption. Why, they wondered, should economic activity exist outside of this model? Barry Commoner's work was among the most influential at an early stage in this debate. He is concerned with technological society and how it can be modified so as not to act as a parasite on the natural environment. In The Closing Circle, *Commoner recast the inhabited earth as the "ecosphere"—the systems and organisms that have sustained life for millions of years—and argued that toxic waste from human technology "is a threat to its finely balanced cycles." This excerpt highlights Commoner's argument that modern technology and production methods, not changing patterns of consumption, are the cause of the environmental crisis. Finding technological solutions to environmental problems remains a popular solution among environmentalists, and Commoner became one of the most distinguished advocates of this view.*

New production technologies have displaced old ones. Soap powder has been displaced by synthetic detergents; natural fibers (cotton and wool) have been displaced by synthetic ones; steel and lumber have been displaced by aluminum, plastics, and concrete; railroad freight has been displaced by truck freight; returnable bottles have been displaced by nonreturnable ones. On the road, the low-powered automobile engines of the 1920's and 1930's have been displaced by high-powered ones. On the farm, while per capita production has remained about constant, the amount of harvested acreage has decreased; in effect, fertilizer has displaced land. Older methods of insect control have been displaced by synthetic insecticides, such as DDT, and for

---

Barry Commoner, *The Closing Circle: Nature, Man, and Technology* (New York: Alfred A. Knopf, 1971), 144–46, 163–64, 176–77.

controlling weeds the cultivator has been displaced by the herbicide spray. Range-feeding of livestock has been displaced by feedlots.

In each of these cases, what has changed drastically is the technology of production rather than over-all output of the economic good. Of course, part of the economic growth in the United States since 1946 has been based on some newly introduced goods: air conditioners, television sets, tape recorders, and snowmobiles, all of which have increased absolutely without displacing an older product. . . . In general, the growth of the United States economy since 1946 has had a surprisingly small effect on the degree to which individual needs for basic economic goods have been met. That statistical fiction, the "average American," now consumes, each year, about as many calories, protein, and other foods (although somewhat less of vitamins); uses about the same amount of clothes and cleaners; occupies about the same amount of newly constructed housing; requires about as much freight; and drinks about the same amount of beer (twenty-six gallons per capita!) as he did in 1946. However, his food is now grown on less land with much more fertilizer and pesticides than before; his clothes are more likely to be made of synthetic fibers than of cotton or wool; he launders with synthetic detergents rather than soap; he lives and works in buildings that depend more heavily on aluminum, concrete, and plastic than on steel and lumber; the goods he uses are increasingly shipped by truck rather than rail; he drinks beer out of nonreturnable bottles or cans rather than out of returnable bottles or at the tavern bar. He is more likely to live and work in air-conditioned surroundings than before. He also drives about twice as far as he did in 1946, in a heavier car, on synthetic rather than natural rubber tires, using more gasoline per mile, containing more tetraethyl lead, fed into an engine of increased horsepower and compression ratio.

These primary changes have led to others. To provide the raw materials needed for the new synthetic fibers, pesticides, detergents, plastics, and rubber, the production of synthetic organic chemicals has also grown very rapidly. The synthesis of organic chemicals uses a good deal of chlorine. Result: chlorine production has increased sharply. To make chlorine, an electric current is passed through a salt solution by way of a mercury electrode. Consequently, mercury consumption for this purpose has increased—by 3,930 per cent in the twenty-five-year postwar period. Chemical products, along with cement for concrete and aluminum (also winners in the growth race), use rather large amounts of electric power. Not surprisingly, then, that item, too, has increased considerably since 1946.

All this reminds us of what we have already been told by advertising—which incidentally has *also* grown; for example, the use of newsprint for advertising has grown faster than its use for news—that we are blessed with an economy based on very modern technologies. What the advertisements do not tell us—as we are urged to buy synthetic shirts and detergents, aluminum furniture, beer in no-return bottles, and Detroit's latest creation—is that *all this "progress" has greatly increased the impact on the environment.*

This pattern of economic growth is the major reason for the environmental crisis. A good deal of the mystery and confusion about the sudden emergence of the environmental crisis can be removed by pinpointing, pollutant by pollutant, how the postwar technological transformation of the United States economy has produced not only the much-heralded 126 per cent rise in GNP, but also, at a rate about ten times faster than the growth of GNP, the rising levels of environmental pollution. . . .

All modern plastics, like synthetic fibers, are composed of manmade, unnatural polymers. They are, therefore, ecologically nondegradable. It is sobering to contemplate the fate of the billions of pounds of plastic already produced. Some of it has of course been burned—thereby adding to the air not only the ordinary products of combustion, but in some cases particular toxic substances such as hydrochloric acid as well. The rest remains, in some form, somewhere on the earth.

Having been designed for their plasticity, the synthetic polymers are easily formed into almost any wanted shape or configuration. Huge numbers of chaotically varied plastic objects have been produced. Apart from the aesthetic consequences, there are serious ecological ones. As the ecosphere is increasingly cluttered with plastic objects nearly infinite in their shape and size, they will—through the workings of nature and the laws of probability—find their way into increasingly narrow nooks and crannies in the natural world. This situation has been poignantly symbolized by a recent photograph of a wild duck, its neck garlanded with a plastic beer-can pack. Consider the awesome improbability of this event. A particular plastic pack is formed in a factory, shipped to a brewer, fitted around six cans of beer, further transported until it reaches human hands that separate plastic from beer can. Then, tossed aside, it nevertheless persists until it comes to float on some woodland lake where a wild duck, too trustingly innocent of modern technology, plunges its head into the plastic noose. . . .

The increase in population accounts for from 12 to 20 per cent of the various increases in total pollutant output since 1946. The affluence factor (i.e., amount of economic good per capita) accounts for from 1 to 5 per cent of the total increase in pollutant output, except in the case of passenger travel, where the contribution rises to about 40 per cent of the total. This reflects a considerable increase in vehicle miles traveled per capita. However, as already pointed out, a good deal of this increase does not reflect improved welfare, but rather the unfortunate need for increased travel incident upon the decay of the inner cities and the growth of suburbs. The technology factor—that is, the increased output of pollutants per unit production resulting from the introduction of new productive technologies since 1946— accounts for about 95 per cent of the total output of pollutants, except in the case of passenger travel, where it accounts for about 40 per cent of the total.

The foregoing conclusions are based on those instances in which quantitative data on pollution output of various productive activities are available. However, from the qualitative evidence on other pollution problems, . . . it is already apparent that they follow a similar pattern: most of the sharp increase in pollution levels is due not so much to population or affluence as to changes in productive technology.

The over-all evidence seems clear. The chief reason for the environmental crisis that has engulfed the United States in recent years is the sweeping transformation of productive technology since World War II. The economy has grown enough to give the United States population about the same amount of basic goods, per capita, as it did in 1946. However, productive technologies with intense impacts on the environment have displaced less destructive ones. The environmental crisis is the inevitable result of this counterecological pattern of growth.

14

The Endangered Species Act

1973

The Endangered Species Act (ESA) was the first law to recognize the inherent value of living animals as part of ecological communities, regardless of any economic value they might have. The members of the House and Senate who passed the bill intended to protect large and symbolic creatures such as bald eagles. They could not have imagined that it would be used to protect the snail darter, a fish thought to be unique to the Little Tennessee River. Ecologists discovered the fish right as the ESA went into effect and only months after a large dam project had been proposed. Opponents of the dam filed suit to stop its construction, claiming that it would cause the extinction of the fish. To supporters, the ESA is a bulwark against projects that place short-term gain ahead of long-term genetic diversity; to opponents, it stands in the way of economic growth.

Sec. 2

(a) FINDINGS. The Congress finds and declares that—

(1) various species of fish, wildlife, and plants in the United States have been rendered extinct as a consequence of economic growth and development untempered by adequate concern and conservation;

(2) other species of fish, wildlife, and plants have been so depleted in numbers that they are in danger of or threatened with extinction;

(3) these species of fish, wildlife, and plants are of aesthetic, ecological, educational, historical, recreational, and scientific value to the Nation and its people;

(4) the United States has pledged itself as a sovereign state in the international community to conserve to the extent practicable the various species of fish or wildlife and plants facing extinction . . .

(5) encouraging the States and other interested parties, through Federal financial assistance and a system of incentives, to develop and maintain conservation programs which meet national and international standards is a key to meeting the Nation's international commitments

Public Law 93-205, Approved December 28, 1973.

and to better safeguarding, for the benefit of all citizens, the Nation's heritage in fish, wildlife, and plants.

(b) PURPOSES. The purposes of this Act are to provide a means whereby the ecosystems upon which endangered species and threatened species depend may be conserved, to provide a program for the conservation of such endangered species and threatened species . . . .

Sec. 3 . . .

The term "endangered species" means any species which is in danger of extinction throughout all or a significant portion of its range other than a species of the Class Insecta determined by the Secretary to constitute a pest whose protection under the provisions of this Act would present an overwhelming and overriding risk to man.

Sec. 4 . . .

BASIS FOR DETERMINATIONS

The Secretary shall make determinations solely on the basis of the best scientific and commercial data available to him after conducting a review of the status of the species and after taking into account those efforts, if any, being made by any State or foreign nation, or any political subdivision of a State or foreign nation, to protect such species, whether by predator control, protection of habitat and food supply, or other conservation practices, within any area under its jurisdiction, or on the high seas.

In carrying out this section, the Secretary shall give consideration to species which have been—

(i) designated as requiring protection from unrestricted commerce by any foreign nation, or pursuant to any international agreement; or

(ii) identified as in danger of extinction, or likely to become so within the foreseeable future, by any State agency or by any agency of a foreign nation that is responsible for the conservation of fish or wildlife or plants.

(2) The Secretary shall designate critical habitat, and make revisions thereto, under subsection (a)(3) on the basis of the best scientific data available and after taking into consideration the economic impact, and any other relevant impact, of specifying any particular area as critical habitat. The Secretary may exclude any area from critical habitat if he determines that the benefits of such exclusion outweigh the benefits of specifying such area as part of the critical

habitat, unless he determines, based on the best scientific and commercial data available, that the failure to designate such area as critical
habitat will result in the extinction of the species concerned.

15

BILL DEVALL AND GEORGE SESSIONS

On Cultivating Ecological Consciousness

1985

*Bill Devall and George Sessions follow biocentric philosophy to its
absolute limit.* In Deep Ecology, *they argue that humans have no right
to appropriate any more from the natural world than they need for survival. The idea originated with the Norwegian thinker Arne Naess, who
conceived of deep ecology as a philosophy that would move modern culture toward a mutual flourishing of human and nonhuman life, resulting in harmony and equilibrium. Naess believed that people could learn
deep lessons from experience and that reflection would lead to a sense of
wholeness and unity. In the United States, however, deep ecology became
an example of the radical response of the 1980s, when environmentalists
reacted to the conservative backlash represented by President Ronald
Reagan's domestic policies. The severity of deep ecology isolated it from
any political process, and further isolated environmentalism from a public still sympathetic to its basic goals.*

Deep ecology is emerging as a way of developing a new balance and
harmony between individuals, communities and all of Nature. It can
potentially satisfy our deepest yearnings: faith and trust in our most
basic intuitions; courage to take direct action; joyous confidence to
dance with the sensuous harmonies discovered through spontaneous,
playful intercourse with the rhythms of our bodies, the rhythms of
flowing water, changes in the weather and seasons, and the overall

Bill Devall and George Sessions, *Deep Ecology: Living as If Nature Mattered* (Salt Lake
City: Peregrine Smith Books, 1985), 7–9, 67–70.

processes of life on Earth. We invite you to explore the vision that deep ecology offers.

The deep ecology movement involves working on ourselves, what poet-philosopher Gary Snyder calls "the real work," the work of really looking at ourselves, of becoming more real.

This is the work we call cultivating ecological consciousness. This process involves becoming more aware of the actuality of rocks, wolves, trees, and rivers—the cultivation of the insight that everything is connected. Cultivating ecological consciousness is a process of learning to appreciate silence and solitude and rediscovering how to listen. It is learning how to be more receptive, trusting, holistic in perception, and is grounded in a vision of nonexploitive science and technology.

This process involves being honest with ourselves and seeking clarity in our intuitions, then acting from clear principles. It results in taking charge of our actions, taking responsibility, practicing self-discipline and working honestly within our community. It is simple but not easy work. Henry David Thoreau, nineteenth-century naturalist and writer, admonishes us, "Let your life be a friction against the machine." . . .

We believe that humans have a vital need to cultivate ecological consciousness and that this need is related to the needs of the planet. At the same time, humans need direct contact with untrammeled wilderness, places undomesticated for narrow human purposes.

Many people sense the needs of the planet and the need for wilderness preservation. But they often feel depressed or angry, impotent and under stress. They feel they must rely on "the other guy," the "experts." Even in the environmental movement, many people feel that only the professional staff of these organizations can make decisions because they are experts on some technical scientific matters or experts on the complex, convoluted political process. But we need not be technical experts in order to cultivate ecological consciousness. Cultivating ecological consciousness, as Thoreau said, requires that "we front up to the facts and determine to live our lives deliberately, or not at all." We believe that people can clarify their own intuitions, and act from deep principles. . . .

The intuition of biocentric equality is that all things in the biosphere have an equal right to live and blossom and to reach their own individual forms of unfolding and self-realization within the larger Self-realization. This basic intuition is that all organisms and entities in the ecosphere, as parts of the interrelated whole, are equal in intrinsic worth. Naess[2] suggests that biocentric equality as an intuition is true in principle, although in the process of living, all species use each other as food, shelter, etc. Mutual predation is a biological fact of life, and many of the world's religions have struggled with the spiritual implications of this. Some animal liberationists who attempt to sidestep this problem by advocating vegetarianism are forced to say that the entire plant kingdom including rain forests have no right to their own existence. This evasion flies in the face of the basic intuition of equality. Aldo Leopold expressed this intuition when he said humans are "plain citizens" of the biotic community, not lord and master over all other species.

Biocentric equality is intimately related to the all-inclusive Self-realization in the sense that if we harm the rest of Nature then we are harming ourselves. There are no boundaries and everything is inter-related. But insofar as we perceive things as individual organisms or entities, the insight draws us to respect all human and nonhuman individuals in their own right as parts of the whole without feeling the need to set up hierarchies of species with humans at the top.

The practical implications of this intuition or norm suggest that we should live with minimum rather than maximum impact on other species and on the Earth in general. Thus we see another aspect of our guiding principle: "simple in means, rich in ends." . . .

Basic Principles

1. The well-being and flourishing of human and nonhuman Life on Earth have value in themselves (synonyms: intrinsic value, inherent value). These values are independent of the usefulness of the nonhuman world for human purposes.

2. Richness and diversity of life forms contribute to the realization of these values and are also values in themselves.

3. Humans have no right to reduce this richness and diversity except to satisfy *vital* needs.

4. The flourishing of human life and cultures is compatible with a substantial decrease of the human population. The flourishing of nonhuman life requires such a decrease.

---

[2]Arne Naess (b. 1912), Norwegian philosopher and founder of deep ecology.

5. Present human interference with the nonhuman world is excessive, and the situation is rapidly worsening.

6. Policies must therefore be changed. These policies affect basic economic, technological, and ideological structures. The resulting state of affairs will be deeply different from the present.

7. The ideological change is mainly that of appreciating *life quality* (dwelling in situations of inherent value) rather than adhering to an increasingly higher standard of living. There will be a profound awareness of the difference between big and great.

8. Those who subscribe to the foregoing points have an obligation directly or indirectly to try to implement the necessary changes.

16

INTERGOVERNMENTAL PANEL ON CLIMATE CHANGE

Summary for Policymakers
2001

Upon its creation in 1988, the Intergovernmental Panel on Climate Change (IPCC) was charged with creating an authoritative study that would be acceptable to policymakers all over the world as the best possible scientific information on climate change and its causes. The IPCC's most immediate purpose was to provide information for the United Nations Framework Convention on Climate Change, which met in Kyoto, Japan, in December 1997. Delegates to Kyoto agreed on a protocol that would commit the developed countries to decreasing their emissions of greenhouse gases to below 1990 levels (though a number of

Intergovernmental Panel on Climate Change, *Climate Change 2001: The Scientific Basis. Contribution of Working Group I to the Third Assessment Report of the IPCC* (Cambridge: Cambridge University Press, 2001), 2–10.

countries, including the United States, have not ratified the treaty). The report marks a crucial moment in the acceptance of global warming by governments around the world. No organization with the same authority had ever announced a human contribution to climate change.

An Increasing Body of Observations Gives a Collective Picture of a Warming World and Other Changes in the Climate System.

Since the release of the Second Assessment Report (SAR),[3] additional data from new studies of current and palaeoclimates, improved analysis of data sets, more rigorous evaluation of their quality, and comparisons among data from different sources have led to greater understanding of climate change.

THE GLOBAL AVERAGE SURFACE TEMPERATURE HAS INCREASED OVER THE 20TH CENTURY BY ABOUT 0.6°C.

— The global average surface temperature (the average of near surface air temperature over land, and sea surface temperature) has increased since 1861. Over the 20th century the increase has been 0.6 ± 0.2°C. This value is about 0.15°C larger than that estimated by the SAR for the period up to 1994, owing to the relatively high temperatures of the additional years (1995 to 2000) and improved methods of processing the data. These numbers take into account various adjustments, including urban heat island effects. The record shows a great deal of variability; for example, most of the warming occurred during the 20th century, during two periods, 1910 to 1945 and 1976 to 2000.

— Globally, it is very likely that the 1990s was the warmest decade and 1998 the warmest year in the instrumental record, since 1861.

— New analyses of proxy data for the Northern Hemisphere indicate that the increase in temperature in the 20th century is likely to have been the largest of any century during the past 1,000 years. It is also likely that, in the Northern Hemisphere,

[3]The Second Assessment Report of the IPCC (1996).

the 1990s was the warmest decade and 1998 the warmest year. Because less data are available, less is known about annual averages prior to 1,000 years before present and for conditions prevailing in most of the Southern Hemisphere prior to 1861. . . .

TEMPERATURES HAVE RISEN DURING THE PAST FOUR DECADES IN THE LOWEST 8 KILOMETRES OF THE ATMOSPHERE.

—Since the late 1950s (the period of adequate observations from weather balloons), the overall global temperature increases in the lowest 8 kilometres of the atmosphere and in surface temperature have been similar at 0.1°C per decade.

—Since the start of the satellite record in 1979, both satellite and weather balloon measurements show that the global average temperature of the lowest 8 kilometres of the atmosphere has changed by +0.05 ± 0.10°C per decade, but the global average surface temperature has increased significantly by +0.15 ± 0.05°C per decade. The difference in the warming rates is statistically significant. This difference occurs primarily over the tropical and sub-tropical regions. . . .

SNOW COVER AND ICE EXTENT HAVE DECREASED.

—Satellite data show that there are very likely to have been decreases of about 10% in the extent of snow cover since the late 1960s, and ground-based observations show that there is very likely to have been a reduction of about two weeks in the annual duration of lake and river ice cover in the mid- and high latitudes of the Northern Hemisphere, over the 20th century.

—There has been a widespread retreat of mountain glaciers in non-polar regions during the 20th century.

—Northern Hemisphere spring and summer sea-ice extent has decreased by about 10 to 15% since the 1950s. It is likely that there has been about a 40% decline in Arctic sea-ice thickness during late summer to early autumn in recent decades and a considerably slower decline in winter sea-ice thickness.

GLOBAL AVERAGE SEA LEVEL HAS RISEN AND OCEAN HEAT CONTENT HAS INCREASED.

—Tide gauge data show that global average sea level rose between 0.1 and 0.2 metres during the 20th century.

— Global ocean heat content has increased since the late 1950s, the period for which adequate observations of sub-surface ocean temperatures have been available. . . .

Emissions of Greenhouse Gases and Aerosols Due to Human Activities Continue to Alter the Atmosphere in Ways That Are Expected to Affect the Climate.

Changes in climate occur as a result of both internal variability within the climate system and external factors (both natural and anthropogenic).[4] The influence of external factors on climate can be broadly compared using the concept of radiative forcing.[5] A positive radiative forcing, such as that produced by increasing concentrations of greenhouse gases, tends to warm the surface. A negative radiative forcing, which can arise from an increase in some types of aerosols (microscopic airborne particles) tends to cool the surface. Natural factors, such as changes in solar output or explosive volcanic activity, can also cause radiative forcing. Characterisation of these climate forcing agents and their changes over time is required to understand past climate changes in the context of natural variations and to project what climate changes could lie ahead. . . .

There Is New and Stronger Evidence That Most of the Warming Observed over the Last 50 Years Is Attributable to Human Activities.

The SAR concluded: "The balance of evidence suggests a discernible human influence on global climate." That report also noted that the anthropogenic signal was still emerging from the background of natural climate variability. Since the SAR, progress has been made in reducing uncertainty, particularly with respect to distinguishing and quantifying the magnitude of responses to different external influences. Although many of the sources of uncertainty identified in the SAR still remain to some degree, new evidence and improved understanding support an updated conclusion.

— There is a longer and more closely scrutinised temperature record and new model estimates of variability. The warming

---

[4] Relating to or resulting from the influence humans have on the natural world.
[5] Any climatic alteration or imbalance leading to a greater (positive forcing) or lesser (negative forcing) intensity of solar radiation on the earth's surface.

over the past 100 years is very unlikely to be due to internal variability alone, as estimated by current models. Reconstructions of climate data for the past 1,000 years also indicate that this warming was unusual and is unlikely to be entirely natural in origin.

—There are new estimates of the climate response to natural and anthropogenic forcing, and new detection techniques have been applied. Detection and attribution studies consistently find evidence for an anthropogenic signal in the climate record of the last 35 to 50 years. . . .

—The warming over the last 50 years due to anthropogenic greenhouse gases can be identified despite uncertainties in forcing due to anthropogenic sulphate aerosol and natural factors (volcanoes and solar irradiance). The anthropogenic sulphate aerosol forcing, while uncertain, is negative over this period and therefore cannot explain the warming. Changes in natural forcing during most of this period are also estimated to be negative and are unlikely to explain the warming. . . .

—Most of these studies find that, over the last 50 years, the estimated rate and magnitude of warming due to increasing concentrations of greenhouse gases alone are comparable with, or larger than, the observed warming. Furthermore, most model estimates that take into account both greenhouse gases and sulphate aerosols are consistent with observations over this period. . . .

In the light of new evidence and taking into account the remaining uncertainties, most of the observed warming over the last 50 years is likely to have been due to the increase in greenhouse gas concentrations.

Furthermore, it is very likely that the 20th century warming has contributed significantly to the observed sea level rise, through thermal expansion of sea water and widespread loss of land ice. Within present uncertainties, observations and models are both consistent with a lack of significant acceleration of sea level rise during the 20th century.

17

EDWARD O. WILSON

To the Ends of the Earth

2002

Biological diversity refers to the richness of life on the planet — the number of species — and also to the richness of genetic information within species. Natural scientists began to use the concept as a measure of ecosystem health in the 1980s in response to increasing species endangerment and extinction reported from regions all over the world. Edward O. Wilson, one of the most respected biologists in the United States, expresses the concern that species might be lost before they can even be identified. Popular books such as The Future of Life, *from which this excerpt is taken, reveal the extent to which ecology has become the scientific and policy language of environmentalism.*

The totality of life, known as the biosphere to scientists and creation to theologians, is a membrane of organisms wrapped around Earth so thin it cannot be seen edgewise from a space shuttle, yet so internally complex that most species composing it remain undiscovered. The membrane is seamless. From Everest's peak to the floor of the Mariana Trench,[6] creatures of one kind or another inhabit virtually every square inch of the planetary surface. They obey the fundamental principle of biological geography, that wherever there is liquid water, organic molecules, and an energy source, there is life. Given the near-universality of organic materials and energy of some kind or other, water is the deciding element on planet Earth. It may be no more than a transient film on grains of sand, it may never see sunlight, it may be boiling hot or supercooled, but there will be some kind of organism living in or upon it. Even if nothing alive is visible to the naked eye, single cells of microorganisms will be growing and reproducing there,

---

[6]The lowest region on the Earth's surface, 36,210 feet below sea level at its deepest point. It is located 200 miles east of the Mariana Islands, in the northwestern Pacific Ocean.

Edward O. Wilson, *The Future of Life* (New York: Alfred A. Knopf, 2002), 3, 10–21.

or at least dormant and awaiting the arrival of liquid water to kick them back into activity. . . .

Studies of the distribution of life have revealed several fundamental patterns in the way species proliferate and are fitted together in Earth's far-flung ecosystems. The first, the most elementary, is that bacteria and archaeans[7] occur everywhere there is life of any kind, whether on the surface or deep beneath it. The second is that, if there is even the smallest space through which to wriggle or swim, tiny protists[8] and invertebrates invade and proceed to prey on the microbes and one another. The third principle is that the more space available, up to and including the largest ecosystems such as grasslands and oceans, the larger are the largest animals living in them. And finally, the greatest diversity of life, as measured by the number of species, occurs in habitats with the most year-round solar energy, the widest exposure of ice-free terrain, the most varied terrain, and the greatest climatic stability across long stretches of time. Thus the equatorial rainforests of the Asian, African, and South American continents possess by far the largest number of plant and animal species.

Regardless of its magnitude, biodiversity (short for biological diversity) is everywhere organized into three levels. At the top are the ecosystems, such as rainforests, coral reefs, and lakes. Next are the species, composed of the organisms in the ecosystems, from algae and swallowtail butterflies to moray eels and people. At the bottom are the variety of genes making up the heredity of individuals that compose each of the species.

Every species is bound to its community in the unique manner by which it variously consumes, is consumed, competes, and cooperates with other species. It also indirectly affects the community in the way it alters the soil, water, and air. The ecologist sees the whole as a network of energy and material continuously flowing into the community from the surrounding physical environment, and back out, and then on round to create the perpetual ecosystem cycles on which our own existence depends.

It is easy to visualize an ecosystem, especially if it is as physically discrete as, say, a marsh or an alpine meadow. But does its dynamical

[7]One of the three domains of life, including eukaryota (consisting of plants, animals, fungi, and protists), bacteria, and archaea. Archaea live in extreme environments, such as hot springs, ocean vents, and the intestines of animals.

[8]Protists are a category of life consisting of microbes such as slime molds, protozoa, and algae.

network of organisms, materials, and energy link it to other eco-systems? In 1972 the British inventor and scientist James E. Lovelock said that, in fact, it is tied to the entire biosphere, which can be thought of as a kind of superorganism that surrounds the planet. This singular entity he called Gaia, after Gaea, or Ge, a vaguely personal goddess of early Greece, giver of dreams, divine personification of Earth, and object of the cult of Earth, as well as mother of the seas, the mountains, and the twelve Titans—in other words, *big*. There is considerable merit in looking at life in this grand holistic manner. Alone among the solar planets, Earth's physical environment is held by its organisms in a delicate equilibrium utterly different from what would be the case in their absence. There is plenty of evidence that even some individual species have a measurable global impact. In the most notable example, the oceanic phytoplankton, composed of micro-scopic, photosynthesizing bacteria, archaeans, and algae, is a major player in the control of the world climate. Dimethylsulfide generated by the algae alone is believed to be an important factor in the regula-tion of cloud formation.

The concept of the biosphere as Gaia has two versions: strong and weak. The strong version holds that the biosphere is a true superor-ganism, with each of the species in it optimized to stabilize the envi-ronment and benefit from balance in the entire system, like cells of the body or workers of an ant colony. This is a lovely metaphor, with a kernel of truth, providing the idea of superorganism is broadened enough. The strong version, however, is generally rejected by biolo-gists, including Lovelock himself, as a working principle. The weak version, on the other hand, which holds that some species exercise widespread and even global influence, is well substantiated. Its accep-tance has stimulated important new programs of research. . . .

How many species are there in the world? Somewhere between 1.5 and 1.8 million have been discovered and given a formal scientific name. No one has yet made an exact count from the taxonomic litera-ture published over the past 250 years. We know this much, however: the roster, whatever its length, is but a mere beginning. Estimates of the true number of living species range, according to the method used, from 3.6 million to 100 million or more. The median of the esti-mates is a little over 10 million, but few experts would risk their repu-tations by insisting on this figure or any other, even to the nearest million.

The truth is that we have only begun to explore life on Earth. How little we know is epitomized by bacteria of the genus *Prochlorococcus*, arguably the most abundant organisms on the planet and responsible for a large part of the organic production of the ocean—yet unknown to science until 1988. *Prochlorococcus* cells float passively in open water at 70,000 to 200,000 per milliliter, multiplying with energy captured from sunlight. Their extremely small size is what makes them so elusive. They belong to a special group called picoplankton, forms even smaller than conventional bacteria and barely visible even at the highest optical magnification.

The blue ocean teems with other novel and little-known bacteria, archaeans, and protozoans. When researchers began to focus on them in the 1990s, they discovered that these organisms are vastly more abundant and diverse than anyone had previously imagined. Much of this miniature world exists in and around previously unseen dark matter, composed of wispy aggregates of colloids, cell fragments, and polymers that range in diameter from billionths to hundredths of a meter. Some of the material contains "hot spots" of nutrients that attract scavenger bacteria and their tiny bacterial and protozoan predators. The ocean we peer into, seemingly clear with only an occasional fish and invertebrate passing beneath, is not the ocean we thought. The visible organisms are just the tip of a vast biomass pyramid.

Among the multicellular organisms of Earth in all environments, the smallest species are also the least known. Of the fungi, which are nearly as ubiquitous as the microbes, 69,000 species have been identified and named, but as many as 1.6 million are thought to exist. Of the nematode worms, making up four of every five animals on Earth and the most widely distributed, 15,000 species are known, but millions more may await discovery. . . .

One of the open frontiers in biodiversity exploration is the floor of the ocean, which from surf to abyss covers 70 percent of Earth's surface. All of the thirty-six known animal phyla, the highest-ranking and most inclusive groups in the taxonomic hierarchy, occur there, as opposed to only ten on the land. Among the most familiar are the Arthropoda, or the insects, crustaceans, spiders, and their sundry relations; and the Mollusca, comprising the snails, mussels, and octopuses. Amazingly, two marine phyla have been discovered during the past thirty years: the Loricifera, miniature bullet-shaped organisms with a girdlelike band around their middle, described for the first time in 1983; and the Cycliophora, plump symbiotic forms that attach themselves to the mouths of lobsters and filter out food particles left over from their hosts' meals, described in 1996. Swarming around the loriciferans and cycliophorans, and deep into the soil of shallow marine waters, are other Alice-in-Wonderland creatures, the meiofauna, most of them barely visible to the naked eye. The strange creatures include gastrotrichs, gnathostomulids, kinorhynchs, tardigrades, chaetognaths, placozoans, and orthonectids, along with nematodes and worm-shaped ciliate protozoans. They can be found in buckets of sand drawn from the intertidal surf and offshore shallow water around the world. So, for those seeking a new form of recreation, plan a day at the nearest beach. Take an umbrella, bucket, trowel, microscope, and illustrated textbook on invertebrate zoology. Don't build sand castles but explore, and as you enjoy this watery microcosm keep in mind what the great nineteenth-century physicist Michael Faraday correctly said, that nothing in this world is too wonderful to be true.

Even the most familiar small organisms are less studied than might be guessed. About ten thousand species of ants are known and named, but that number may double when tropical regions are more fully explored. While recently conducting a study of *Pheidole*, one of the world's two largest ant genera, I uncovered 341 new species, more than doubling the number in the genus and increasing the entire known fauna of ants in the Western Hemisphere by 10 percent. As my monograph went to press in 2001, additional new species were still pouring in, mostly from fellow entomologists collecting in the tropics. . . .

Even the flowering plants, traditionally a favorite of field biologists, retain large pockets of unexamined diversity. About 272,000 species have been described worldwide, but the true number is likely to be 300,000 or more. Each year about 2,000 new species are added to the world list published in botany's standard reference work, the *Index Kewensis*. Even the relatively well-curried United States and Canada continue to yield about 60 new species annually. Some experts believe that as much as 5 percent of the North American flora await discovery, including 300 or more species and races in the biologically rich state of California alone. The novelties are usually rare but not necessarily shy and inconspicuous. Some, like the recently described Shasta snow-wreath (*Neviusia cliftonii*) are flamboyant enough to serve as ornamentals. Many grow in plain sight. A member of the lily family, *Calochortus tiburonensis*, first described in 1972, grows just ten miles from downtown San Francisco. In 1982, a twenty-one-year-old amateur collector, James Morefield, discovered the brand-new leather flower, *Clematis morefieldii*, on the outskirts of Huntsville, Alabama.

Ever deeper rounds of zoological exploration, driven by a sense of urgency over vanishing environments, have revealed surprising numbers of new vertebrates, many of which are placed on the endangered list as soon as they are discovered. The global number of amphibian species, including frogs, toads, salamanders, and the less familiar tropical caecilians, grew between 1985 and 2001 by one third, from 4,003 to 5,282. There can be little doubt that in time it will pass 6,000.

The discovery of new mammals has also continued at a rapid pace. Collectors, by journeying to remote tropical regions and concentrating on small elusive forms such as tenrecs and shrews, have increased the global number in the last two decades from about 4,000 to 5,000. The record for rapid discovery during the past half-century was set by James L. Patton in July 1996. With just three weeks' effort in the central Andes of Colombia, he discovered 6 new species—four mice, a shrew, and a marsupial. Even primates, including apes, monkeys, and lemurs, the most sought of all mammals in the field, are yielding novelties. In the 1990s alone Russell Mittermeier and his colleagues managed to add 9 new species to the 275 previously known. Mittermeier, whose searches take him to tropical forests around the world, estimates that at least another hundred species of primates await discovery. . . .

More than half the plant and animal species of the world are believed to occur in the tropical rainforests. From these natural greenhouses, . . . many world records of biodiversity have been reported: 425 kinds of trees in a single hectare (2.5 acres) of Brazil's Atlantic Forest, for example, and 1,300 butterfly species from a corner of Peru's Manu National Park. Both numbers are ten times greater than those from comparable sites in Europe and North America. The record for ants is 365 species from 10 hectares (25 acres) in a forest tract of the upper Peruvian Amazon. I have identified 43 species from the canopy of a single *tree* in the same region, approximately equal to the ant fauna of all the British Isles.

These impressive censuses do not exclude a comparable richness of some groups of organisms in other major environments of the world. A single coral head in Indonesia can harbor hundreds of species of crustaceans, polychaete worms, and other invertebrates, plus a fish or two. Twenty-eight kinds of vines and herbaceous plants have been found growing on a giant *Podocarpus* yellowwood conifer in the temperate rainforest of New Zealand, setting the world record for vascular epiphytes[9] on a single tree. As many as two hundred species of mites, diminutive spiderlike creatures, teem in a single square

---

[9]Plants that grow on top of or are supported by another plant, but do not depend on it for nutrition.

meter of some hardwood forests of North America. In the same spot a gram of soil—a pinch held between thumb and forefinger—contains thousands of species of bacteria. A few are actively multiplying, but most are dormant, each awaiting the special combination of nutrients, moisture, aridity, and temperature to which its particular strain is adapted.

You do not have to visit distant places, or even rise from your seat, to experience the luxuriance of biodiversity. You yourself are a rainforest of a kind. There is a good chance that tiny spiderlike mites build nests at the base of your eyelashes. Fungal spores and hyphae[10] on your toenails await the right conditions to sprout a Lilliputian forest. The vast majority of the cells in your body are not your own; they belong to bacterial and other microorganismic species. More than four hundred such microbial species make their home in your mouth. But rest easy: the bulk of protoplasm you carry around is still human, because microbial cells are so small. Every time you scuff earth or splash mud puddles with your shoes, bacteria, and who knows what else, that are still unknown to science settle on them.

Such is the biospheric membrane that covers Earth, and you and me. It is the miracle we have been given. And our tragedy, because a large part of it is being lost forever before we learn what it is and the best means by which it can be savored and used.

[10]A threadlike part of the vegetative portion of a fungus.

4

Green Politics

18

How to Save the Earth
1970

Between 1968 and 1972, Stewart Brand, a biologist and designer, published the Whole Earth Catalog *as a source of information for how to live independently of industrial society and open what he called "new realms of personal power." Brand set out to give every reader tools "to conduct his own education, find his own inspiration, shape his own environment." The tools he had in mind tended to require little energy to use or capital to build and included camping equipment, homebuilt airplanes, Indian sweat lodges, kick-wheel pottery tables, and birch-bark baby cribs. Following the philosopher and engineer R. Buckminster Fuller, Brant defined a tool as any technology that left natural systems intact and did not create waste. The* Catalog *also gave detailed information on how to purchase government land. It enjoyed a following among those who sought to remove themselves from mainstream society to discover alternative ways of living.*

—Don't use colored facial tissues, paper towels, or toilet paper. The paper dissolves properly in water, but the dye forms a residue.

—If you accumulate coat hangers, don't junk them, return them to the cleaner. Boycott cleaners who won't accept them.

"39 Ways to Save the Earth," *Whole Earth Catalog* (July 1970).

—Use the containers that disintegrate readily. Glass bottles don't decompose. Bottles made of polyvinyl chloride (PVC) give off lethal hydrochloric acid when incinerated. (That's the soft plastic many liquid household cleansers, shampoos and mouthwashes come in. Don't confuse it with stiffer poly-styrene plastic, used mainly for powders.) The Food and Drug Administration has now approved PVC for food packaging too. Don't buy it. Use decomposable—"Biodegradable"—paste-board, cardboard, or paper containers instead. If you can't, *at least* re-employ non-decomposable bottles; don't junk them after one use.

—Don't buy non-returnable containers. When you go to the supermarket for milk, take an empty jug with you. At the check-out stand pour milk from the disposable carton into your recycled jug, give the empty "disposable" carton to the checker, and explain that you must put action on the store because you can't stop buying milk and this is the only way the individual can reach the companies which the store orders from. Hold the aluminum can purchase to a minimum unless you are willing to recycle the aluminum. . . .

—At the gas station, don't let the attendant "top off" your gas tank; this means waste and polluting spillage. The pump should shut off mechanically at the proper amount. (True too for motorboats.)

—If you smoke filter tip cigarettes, don't flush them down the toilet. They'll ruin your plumbing and clog up pumps at the sewage treatment plant. They're practically indestructible. Put them in the garbage.

—Stop smoking.

—Stop littering. Now. If you see a litterbug, object very politely ("Excuse me sir, I think you dropped something."). . . .

—Don't buy or use DDT, DDD, or any other chlorinated hydro-carbon pesticides. The sale of DDT is now illegal in New [M]exico. Do not dispose of DDT or any other poisons down the toilet, in the garbage can, or into a home incinerator or the fireplace. Each of these results in the release of the poison into the environment. . . .

—If you don't really need a car, don't buy a car. Motor vehicles contribute a good half of this country's pollution. Better walk or bicycle. Better for you too.

—If you have to car-commute, don't chug exhaust into the air just for yourself. Form a car pool. Four people in one car put out a quarter the carbon monoxide of four cars.

—Better yet, take a bus to work. Or a train. Per passenger-mile, they pollute air much less than cars. Support mass transit.

—If you still think you need a car of your own, make sure it burns fuel efficiently (i.e., rates high in mpg). Get a low horsepower minimachine for the city, a monster only for lots of freeway driving. . . .

—There's only so much water. Don't leave it running. If it has to be recycled too fast, treatment plants can't purify it properly.

—Measure detergents carefully. If you follow manufacturers' instructions, you'll help cut down a third of all detergent water pollution.

—Since the prime offender in detergent pollution is not suds but phosphates (which encourage algae growth), demand to know how much phosphate is in the detergent you're buying. Write the manufacturer, newspapers, Congressmen, the FDA. Until they let you know, use an unphosphated, nondetergent soap. (Bubble baths, you may be happy to know, do not cause detergent pollution.) . . .

—If you see something wrong and don't know who to contact, bombard newspapers, TV and radio stations with letters. Get friends to join in. Media will help with the message if you're getting nowhere in normal channels. Remember: publicity hurts polluters.

—Help get antipollution ideas into kids' heads. If you're a teacher, a Scout leader, a camp couns[e]lor, a summer playground assistant, teach children about litter, conservation, noise . . . about being considerate, which is what it all comes down to.

—If you're in a relatively rural area, save vegetable wastes (sawdust, corn husks, cardboard, table scraps, et al.) in a compost heap instead of throwing them out. Eventually you can spread it as fertilizer—nature's way of recycling garbage.

—Remember: All Power Pollutes. Especially gas and electric power, which either smog up the air or dirty the rivers. So cut down on power consumption. In winter, put the furnace a few degrees lower (it's healthier) and wear a sweater. . . .

—Protesting useless pollution? Don't wear indestructible metal buttons that say so.

—Fight to keep noise at a minimum between 11 p.m. and 7 a.m. Studies show that sounds which aren't loud enough to wake you can still break your dream cycle—so you awaken tired and cranky. By the same token, be kind to neighbors. Suggest that your local radio/TV station remind listeners at 10 p.m. to turn down the volume.

—When you shop, take a reusable tote with you as Europeans do—and don't accept excess packaging and paper bags. The packaging you take home today becomes trash tomorrow. This is costing you in terms of dollars and health. Packaging can be deceptive, disguising product contents. Packaging increases the cost of the products you buy. By converting trees to paper, it upsets the forest life-cycle. You must pay high municipal taxes for trash disposal. . . .

—Patronize stores that specialize in unpesticided, organically-grown food in biodegradable containers. There's probably such a health food store near you.

—Radicalize your community. Do something memorable on April 22nd, the date of the First National Environment Teach-In. One group's given Polluter of the Week awards to deserving captains of industry. In traffic jams, other groups have handed out leaflets titled "Don't You Feel Stupid Sitting Here?" which list advantages of car pools and mass transit. . . .

—Last, and most important—vitally important—if you want more than two children, adopt them. You know all the horror stories. They're true. Nightmarishly true. And that goes for the whole American economy. Unless we can stop fanatically producing and consuming more than we need, we won't have a world to stand on. Care! Who will, if we don't?

19

DENIS HAYES

Earth Day

1970

Earth Day, held for the first time on April 22, 1970, attracted an un-precedented cross-section of the citizenry, suggesting that the environment had become a popular political issue. But the event cannot be separated from the protest of the Vietnam War going on at the same time. The student organizers of Earth Day, like Denis Hayes, used the same tactics developed to resist the war to attack corporations and the government for failing to control pollution and waste. Rather than being satisfied with limited aims like government regulation, students considered Earth Day the beginning of a movement aimed at revolutionizing American society. Politicians warned of the supposed economic costs and social sacrifices of regulation. Ten years later, the tensions and divisions between activists and politicians present at the first Earth Day entered national politics when Ronald Reagan entered the White House.

I suspect that the politicians and businessmen who are jumping on the environmental bandwagon don't have the slightest idea what they are getting into. They are talking about filters on smokestacks while we are challenging corporate irresponsibility. They are bursting with pride about plans for totally inadequate municipal sewage treatment plants; we are challenging the ethics of a society that, with only 6 percent of the world's population, accounts for more than half of the world's annual consumption of raw materials.

Our country is stealing from poorer nations and from generations yet unborn. We seem to have a reverse King Midas touch. Everything we touch turns to garbage—142 tons of smoke, 7 million junked cars, 30 million tons of paper, 28 billion bottles, 48 billion cans each year. We waste riches in planned obsolescence and invest the overwhelm-

---

Denis Hayes, "The Beginning," in Steve Cotton, ed., *Earth Day—The Beginning* (New York: Bantam Books, 1970), xiii–xv.

ing bulk of our national budget in ABMs and MIRVs[1] and other means of death. Russia can destroy every American twelve times; America can destroy every Russian forty times. I guess that is supposed to mean that we are ahead.

We're spending insanely large sums on military hardware instead of eliminating hunger and poverty. We squander our resources on moon dust while people live in wretched housing. We still waste lives and money on a war that we should never have entered and should get out of immediately.

We have made Vietnam an ecological catastrophe. Vietnam was once capable of producing a marketable surplus of grain. Now America must feed her. American bombs have pockmarked Vietnam with more than 2.6 million craters a year, some of them thirty feet deep. We spent $73 million on defoliation in Vietnam last year alone, much of it on 2,4,5-T, a herbicide we've now found causes birth defects. We dumped defoliants on Vietnam at the rate of 10,000 pounds a month, and in the last fiscal year alone we blackened 6,600 square miles. We cannot pretend to be concerned with the environment of this or any other country as long as we continue the war in Vietnam or wage war in Cambodia, Laos, or anywhere else.

But even if that war were over tomorrow, we would still be killing this planet. We are systematically destroying our land, our streams, and our seas. We foul our air, deaden our senses, and pollute our bodies. And it's getting worse.

America's political and business institutions don't seem yet to have realized that some of us want to live in this country thirty years from now. They had better come to recognize it soon. We don't have very much time. We cannot afford to give them very much time.

When it comes to salvaging the environment, the individual is almost powerless. You can pick up litter, and if you're diligent, you may be able to find some returnable bottles. But you are forced to breathe the lung-corroding poison which companies spew into the air. You cannot buy electricity from a power company which does not pollute. You cannot find products in biodegradable packages. You cannot even look to the manufacturer for reliable information on the ecological effects of a product.

You simply can't live an ecologically sound life in America. That is

---

[1]ABM stands for anti-ballistic missiles. MIRV stands for multiple independently targetable reentry vehicles.

not one of the options open to you. Go shopping and you find dozens of laundry products; it seems like a tremendous array unless you know that most are made by three companies, and the differences in cleaning power are almost negligible. If you really want to be ecologically sound, you won't buy any detergents—just some old-fashioned laundry soap and a bit of soda. But there's nothing on those packages to tell you the phosphate content, and there's nothing in the supermarket to tell you, only meaningless advertising that keeps dunning you.

We are learning. In response, industry has turned the environmental problem over to its public relations men. We've been deluged with full-page ads about pollution problems and what's being done about them. It would appear from most of them that things are fine and will soon be perfect. But the people of America are still coughing. And our eyes are running, and our lungs are blackening, and our property is corroding, and we're getting angry. We're getting angry at half-truths, angry at semitruths, and angry at outright lies.

We are tired of being told that we are to blame for corporate depredations. Political and business leaders once hoped that they could turn the environmental movement into a massive antilitter campaign. They have failed. We have learned not to place our faith in regulatory agencies that are supposed to act in the public interest. We have learned not to believe the advertising that sells us presidents the way it sells us useless products.

We will not appeal any more to the conscience of institutions because institutions have no conscience. If we want them to do what is right, we must make them do what is right. We will use proxy fights, lawsuits, demonstrations, research, boycotts, ballots—whatever it takes. This may be our last chance. If environment is a fad, it's going to be our last fad.

Things as we know them are falling apart. There is an unease across this country today. People know that something is wrong. The war is part of it, but most critics of the war have, from the beginning, known that the war is only a symptom of something much deeper. Poor people have long known what is wrong. Now the alley garbage, the crowding and the unhappiness and the crime have spread beyond the ghetto and a whole society is coming to realize that it must drastically change course.

We are building a movement, a movement with a broad base, a movement which transcends traditional political boundaries. It is a movement that values people more than technology, people more than political boundaries and political ideologies, people more than profit. It will be a difficult fight. Earth Day is the beginning.

20

ERNEST CALLENBACH

Ecotopia

1975

---

*Novelist Ernest Callenbach imagined a transformation in the entire
political and material basis of American society in the form of a new
nation, born in bloody civil war and founded on a "new biology-conscious
philosophy." His novel* Ecotopia *is about this revolution. Twenty years
after Oregon, Washington, and northern California declare their independence from the United States to form their own commonwealth, journalist William Weston travels to Ecotopia to observe life there. The novel
consists of the notebook Weston kept during that visit. Through this fictional device, Callenbach creates a world of complete equality, but also
one in which a nationally unifying solution to the problem of the environment proved to be impossible. This excerpt focuses on the mood of
post-secession San Francisco.*

San Francisco, May 5. As I emerged from the train terminal into the
streets, I had little idea what to expect from this city—which had once
proudly boasted of rising from its own ashes after a terrible earth-
quake and fire. San Francisco was once known as "America's favorite
city" and had an immense appeal to tourists. Its dramatic hills and
bridges, its picturesque cable cars, and its sophisticated yet relaxed
people had drawn visitors who returned again and again. Would I find
that it still deserves its reputation as an elegant and civilized place?

I checked my bag and set out to explore a bit. The first shock hit
me at the moment I stepped onto the street. There was a strange hush
over everything. I expected to encounter something at least a little
like the exciting bustle of our cities—cars honking, taxis swooping,
clots of people pushing about in the hurry of urban life. What I found,
when I had gotten over my surprise at the quiet, was that Market
Street, once a mighty boulevard striking through the city down to the

---

Ernest Callenbach, *Ecotopia* (Berkeley, Calif.: Banyan Tree Books, 1975), 10–13.

waterfront, has become a mall planted with thousands of trees. The "street" itself, on which electric taxis, minibuses, and deliverycarts purr along, has shrunk to a two-lane affair. The remaining space, which is huge, is occupied by bicycle lanes, fountains, sculptures, kiosks, and absurd little gardens surrounded by benches. Over it all hangs the almost sinister quiet, punctuated by the whirr of bicycles and cries of children. There is even the occasional song of a bird, unbelievable as that may seem on a capital city's crowded main street.

Scattered here and there are large conical-roofed pavilions, with a kiosk in the center selling papers, comic books, magazines, fruit juices, and snacks. (Also cigarettes—the Ecotopians have *not* managed to stamp out smoking!) The pavilions turn out to be stops on the minibus system, and people wait there out of the rain. These buses are comical battery-driven contraptions, resembling the antique cable cars that San Franciscans were once so fond of. They are driverless, and are steered and stopped by an electronic gadget that follows wires buried in the street. (A safety bumper stops them in case someone fails to get out of the way.) To enable people to get on and off quickly, during the 15 seconds the bus stops, the floor is only a few inches above ground level; the wheels are at the extreme ends of the vehicle. Rows of seats face outward, so on a short trip you simply sit down momentarily, or stand and hang onto one of the hand grips. In bad weather fringed fabric roofs can be extended outward to provide more shelter. . . .

The bucolic atmosphere of the new San Francisco can perhaps best be seen in the fact that, down Market Street and some other streets, creeks now run. These had earlier, at great expense, been put into huge culverts underground, as is usual in cities. The Ecotopians spent even more to bring them up to ground level again. So now on this major boulevard you may see a charming series of little falls, with water gurgling and splashing, and channels lined with rocks, trees, bamboos, ferns. There even seem to be minnows in the water—though how they are kept safe from marauding children and cats, I cannot guess.

Despite the quiet, the streets are full of people, though not in Manhattan densities. (Some foot traffic has been displaced to lacy bridges which connect one skyscraper to another, sometimes 15 or 20 stories up.) Since practically the whole street area is "sidewalk," nobody worries about obstructions—or about the potholes which, as they develop in the pavement, are planted with flowers. I came across a group of street musicians playing Bach, with a harpsichord and a half dozen other instruments. There are vendors of food pushing gaily colored carts that offer hot snacks, chestnuts, ice cream. Once I even saw a juggler and magician team, working a crowd of children—it reminded me of some medieval movie. And there are many strollers, gawkers, and loiterers—people without visible business who simply take the street for granted as an extension of their living rooms. Yet, despite so many unoccupied people, the Ecotopian streets seem ridiculously lacking in security gates, doormen, guards, or other precautions against crime. And no one seems to feel our need for automobiles to provide protection in moving from place to place.

I had noticed on the train that Ecotopian clothes tend to be very loose, with bright colors striving to make up for what is lacking in style and cut. This impression is confirmed now that I have observed thousands of San Franciscans. The typical Ecotopian man wears non-descript trousers (even denim is common—perhaps from nostalgia for American fashions of the pre-secession decades?) topped with an often hideous shirt, sweater, poncho, or jacket. Despite the usually chilly weather, sandals are common among both sexes. The women often wear pants also, but loose-flowing gypsy-like skirts are more usual. A few people wear outlandish skin-tight garments which look like diving wet-suits, but are woven of some fabric unknown to me. They may be members of some special group, as their attire is so unusual. Leather and furs seem to be favorite materials—they are used for purses and pouches, pants and jackets. Children wear miniature versions of adult clothing; there seem to be no special outfits for them.

Ecotopians setting out to go more than a block or two usually pick up one of the sturdy white-painted bicycles that lie about the streets by the hundreds and are available free to all. Dispersed by the movements of citizens during the day and evening, they are returned by night crews to the places where they will be needed the next day. When I remarked to a friendly pedestrian that this system must be a joy to thieves and vandals, he denied it heatedly. He then put a case, which may not be totally far-fetched, that it is cheaper to lose a few bicycles than to provide more taxis or minibuses.

Ecotopians, I am discovering, spout statistics on such questions with reckless abandon. They have a way of introducing "social costs" into their calculations which inevitably involves a certain amount of optimistic guesswork. It would be interesting to confront such informants with one of the hard-headed experts from our auto or highway industries—who would, of course, be horrified by the Ecotopians' abolition of cars.

21

AMORY LOVINS

Soft Energy

1977

In 1976, physicist Amory Lovins published an article called "Energy Strategy: The Road Not Taken?" in the journal Foreign Affairs. *The nonprofit environmental organization Friends of the Earth published a book-length version under the title* Soft Energy Paths *the following year. Lovins set out to demolish the assumption, popular among energy planners of the 1970s, that increasing energy consumption is the basis of increasing prosperity. Instead, he proposed "soft" technology, especially solar energy, as a way of fostering an ecologically sound and economically just society. Soft energy appealed to environmentalists because it decentralized political power by allowing for multiple points of power generation and it had none of the dangers of nuclear power, which environmentalists opposed throughout the 1970s. Lovins looked forward to a solar economy—using the sun as the energy base for all economic activity.*

There exists today a body of energy technologies that have certain specific features in common and that offer great technical, economic and political attractions, yet for which there is no generic term. For lack of a more satisfactory term, I shall call them "soft" technologies: a textural description, intended to mean not vague, mushy, speculative or ephemeral, but rather flexible, resilient, sustainable and benign. Energy paths dependent on soft technologies will be called "soft" energy paths, as the "hard" technologies . . . constitute a "hard" path (in both senses). The distinction between hard and soft energy paths rests not on how much energy is used, but on the technical and sociopolitical *structure* of the energy system, thus focusing our attention on consequent and crucial political differences.

The social structure is significantly shaped by the rapid deployment of soft technologies. These are defined by five characteristics:

Amory B. Lovins, "Energy Strategy: The Road Not Taken?" *Foreign Affairs*, 55 (October 1976): 65–96.

—They rely on renewable energy flows that are always there whether we use them or not, such as sun and wind and vegetation: on energy income, not on depletable energy capital.

—They are diverse, so that energy supply is an aggregate of very many individually modest contributions, each designed for maximum effectiveness in particular circumstances.

—They are flexible and relatively low-technology—which does not mean unsophisticated, but rather, easy to understand and use without esoteric skills, accessible rather than arcane.

—They are matched in *scale* and in geographic distribution to end-use needs, taking advantage of the free distribution of most natural energy flows.

—They are matched in *energy quality* to end-use needs: a key feature. . . .

A feature of soft technologies as essential as their fitting end-use needs (for a different reason) is their appropriate scale, which can achieve important types of economies not available to larger, more centralized systems. This is done in five ways, of which the first is reducing and sharing overheads. Roughly half your electricity bill is fixed distribution costs to pay the overheads of a sprawling energy system: transmission lines, transformers, cables, meters and people to read them, planners, headquarters, billing computers, interoffice memos, advertising agencies. For electrical and some fossil-fuel systems, distribution accounts for more than half of total capital cost, and administration for a significant fraction of total operating cost. Local or domestic energy systems can reduce or even eliminate these infrastructure costs. The resulting savings can far outweigh the extra costs of the dispersed maintenance infrastructure that the small systems require, particularly where that infrastructure already exists or can be shared (e.g., plumbers fixing solar heaters as well as sinks).

Small scale brings further savings by virtually eliminating distribution losses, which are cumulative and pervasive in centralized energy systems (particularly those using high-quality energy). Small systems also avoid direct diseconomies of scale,[2] such as the frequent unreliability of large units and the related need to provide instant "spinning

---

[2]Diseconomies of scale describe a condition in which marginal costs (the cost per unit) increase rather than decrease with increasing output.

reserve" capacity on electrical grids to replace large stations that suddenly fail. Small systems with short lead times greatly reduce exposure to interest, escalation and mistimed demand forecasts—major indirect diseconomies of large scale. . . .

Many genuine soft technologies are now available and are now economic. What are some of them?

Solar heating and, imminently, cooling head the list. They are incrementally cheaper than electric heating, and far more inflation-proof, practically anywhere in the world. In the United States (with fairly high average sunlight levels), they are cheaper than present electric heating virtually anywhere, cheaper than oil heat in many parts, and cheaper than gas and coal in some. Even in the least favorable parts of the continental United States, far more sunlight falls on a typical building than is required to heat and cool it without supplement; whether this is considered economic depends on how the accounts are done. The difference in solar input between the most and least favorable parts of the lower 49 states is generally less than two-fold, and in cold regions, the long heating season can improve solar economics.

Ingenious ways of backfitting existing urban and rural buildings (even large commercial ones) or their neighborhoods with efficient and exceedingly reliable solar collectors are being rapidly developed in both the private and public sectors. In some recent projects, the lead time from ordering to operation has been only a few months. Good solar hardware, often modular, is going into pilot or full-scale production over the next few years, and will increasingly be integrated into buildings as a multipurpose structural element, thereby sharing costs. . . . Some novel types of very simple collectors with far lower costs also show promise in current experiments. Indeed, solar hardware per se is necessary only for backfitting existing buildings. If we build new buildings properly in the first place, they can use "passive" solar collectors—large south windows or glass-covered black south walls—rather than special collectors. If we did this to all new houses in the next 12 years, we would save about as much energy as we expect to recover from the Alaskan North Slope. . . .

Additional soft technologies include wind-hydraulic systems (especially those with a vertical axis), which already seem likely in many design studies to compete with nuclear power in much of North America and Western Europe. But wind is not restricted to making electricity: it can heat, pump, heat-pump, or compress air. Solar process heat, too, is coming along rapidly as we learn to use the 5,800°C. potential of sunlight (much hotter than a boiler). Finally, high- and low-temperature solar collectors, organic converters, and wind machines can form symbiotic hybrid combinations more attractive than the separate components. . . .

Recent research suggests that a largely or wholly solar economy can be constructed in the United States with straightforward soft technologies that are now demonstrated and now economic or nearly economic. Such a conceptual exercise does not require "exotic" methods such as sea-thermal, hot-dry-rock geothermal, cheap (perhaps organic) photovoltaic, or solar-thermal electric systems. If developed, as some probably will be, these technologies could be convenient, but they are in no way essential for an industrial society operating solely on energy income.

22

DAVE FOREMAN

Ecodefense

1985

Dave Foreman, founder of the radical environmental movement Earth First!, published Ecodefense *in 1985 as a compilation of articles from* Earth First! Journal. *The Library of Congress classifies the book under the following subject headings: "Terrorism," "Sabotage," and "Criminal Methods." It lives up to its subtitle as "a field guide to monkeywrenching"—a term for environmental sabotage that originated with Edward Abbey. Perhaps the most famous example, described in this excerpt, is tree spiking, or the practice of inserting long metal nails into trees to dissuade loggers from cutting them. The spikes not only destroy chainsaws, but can be deadly to loggers. With such tactics, radical environmentalists sought to stop the wheels of capitalist development, though without ever challenging the premises of capitalism. Like all sabotage, monkeywrenching rejects political processes and negotiated solutions.*

Dave Foreman and Bill Haywood, eds., *Ecodefense: A Field Guide to Monkeywrenching* (1985; third edition, Chico: Calif.: Abbzug Press, 1993), 8–11, 18–21.

It is time for women and men, individually and in small groups, to act heroically in defense of the wild, to put a monkeywrench into the gears of the machine that is destroying natural diversity. Though illegal, this strategic monkeywrenching can be safe, easy, fun, and—most important—effective in stopping timber cutting, road building, overgrazing, oil and gas exploration, mining, dam building, powerline construction, off-road-vehicle use, trapping, ski area development, and other forms of destruction of the wilderness, as well as cancerous suburban sprawl.

But it must be strategic, it must be thoughtful, it must be deliberate in order to succeed. Such a campaign of resistance would adhere to the following principles:

MONKEYWRENCHING IS NONVIOLENT

Monkeywrenching is nonviolent resistance to the destruction of natural diversity and wilderness. It is never directed against human beings or other forms of life. It is aimed at inanimate machines and tools that are destroying life. Care is always taken to minimize any possible threat to people, including the monkeywrenchers themselves.

MONKEYWRENCHING IS NOT ORGANIZED

There should be no central direction or organization to monkeywrenching. Any type of network would invite infiltration, agents provocateurs, and repression. It is truly individual action. Because of this, communication among monkeywrenchers is difficult and dangerous. Anonymous discussion . . . seems to be the safest avenue of communication to refine techniques, security procedures, and strategy.

MONKEYWRENCHING IS INDIVIDUAL

Monkeywrenching is done by individuals or very small groups of people who have known each other for years. Trust and a good working relationship are essential in such groups. The more people involved, the greater the dangers of infiltration or a loose mouth. Monkeywrenchers avoid working with people they haven't known for a long time, those who can't keep their mouths closed, and those with grandiose or violent ideas (they may be police agents or dangerous crackpots).

MONKEYWRENCHING IS TARGETED

Ecodefenders pick their targets. Mindless, erratic vandalism is counterproductive as well as unethical. Monkeywrenchers know that they do not stop a specific logging sale by destroying any piece of logging equipment they come across. They make sure it belongs to the real culprit. They ask themselves what is the most vulnerable point of a wilderness-destroying project, and strike there. Senseless vandalism leads to loss of popular sympathy.

MONKEYWRENCHING IS TIMELY

There are proper times and places for monkeywrenching. There are also times when monkeywrenching may be counterproductive. Monkeywrenchers generally should not act when there is a nonviolent civil disobedience action—e.g., a blockade—taking place against the opposed project. Monkeywrenching may cloud the issue of direct action, and the blockaders could be blamed for the ecotage and be put in danger from the work crew or police. Blockades and monkeywrenching usually do not mix. Monkeywrenching may also not be appropriate when delicate political negotiations are taking place for the protection of a certain area. There are, of course, exceptions to this rule. The Earth warrior always asks, Will monkeywrenching help or hinder the protection of this place?

MONKEYWRENCHING IS DISPERSED

Monkeywrenching is a widespread movement across the United States. Government agencies and wilderness despoilers from Maine to Hawaii know that their destruction of natural diversity may be resisted. Nationwide monkeywrenching will hasten overall industrial retreat from wild areas.

MONKEYWRENCHING IS DIVERSE

All kinds of people, in all kinds of situations, can be monkeywrenchers. Some pick a large area of wild country, declare it wilderness in their own minds, and resist any intrusion into it. . . . Certain monkeywrenchers may target a specific project, such as a giant powerline, a road under construction, or an oil operation. Some operate in their backyards, while others lie low at home and plan their ecotage a thousand miles away. Some are loners, and others operate in small groups. Even Republicans monkeywrench.

MONKEYWRENCHING IS FUN

Although it is serious and potentially dangerous, monkeywrenching is also fun. There is a rush of excitement, a sense of accomplishment, and unparalleled camaraderie from creeping about in the night resisting those "alien forces from Houston, Tokyo, Washington, DC, and the Pentagon." As Ed Abbey said, "Enjoy, shipmates, enjoy."

MONKEYWRENCHING IS NOT REVOLUTIONARY

Monkeywrenchers do not aim to overthrow any social, political, or economic system. Monkeywrenching is merely nonviolent self-defense of the wild. It is aimed at keeping industrial civilization out of natural areas and causing industry's retreat from areas that should be wild. It is not major industrial sabotage. Explosives, firearms, and other dangerous tools are usually avoided; they invite greater scrutiny from law enforcement agencies, repression, and loss of public support.

MONKEYWRENCHING IS SIMPLE

The simplest possible tool is used. The safest tactic is employed. Elaborate commando operations are generally avoided. The most effective means for stopping the destruction of the wild are often the simplest. There are times when more detailed and complicated operations are necessary. But the monkeywrencher asks, What is the simplest way to do this?

MONKEYWRENCHING IS DELIBERATE AND ETHICAL

Monkeywrenchers are very conscious of the gravity of what they do. They are deliberate about taking such a serious step. They are thoughtful, not cavalier. Monkeywrenchers—although nonviolent— are warriors. They are exposing themselves to possible arrest or injury. It is not a casual or flippant affair. They keep a pure heart and mind about it. They remember that they are engaged in the most moral of all actions: protecting life, defending Earth.

A movement based on the above principles could protect millions of acres of wilderness more stringently than could any congressional act, could insure the propagation of the Grizzly and other threatened life forms better than could an army of game wardens, and could lead to the retreat of industrial civilization from large areas of forest, mountain, desert, prairie, seashore, swamp, tundra, and woodland that are better suited to the maintenance of native diversity than to the production of raw materials for overconsumptive technological human society. . . .

Tree Spiking

Tree spiking can be an extremely effective method of deterring timber sales, and seems to be growing more and more popular. Mill operators are quite wary of accepting timber that may be contaminated with hidden metal objects—saws are expensive, and a "spiked" log can literally bring operations to a screeching halt, at least until a new blade can be put into service. The Forest Service and timber industry are very nervous about spiking—when they or the media raise the subject of monkeywrenching, this is the form most commonly discussed. . . .

There are two basic philosophies of tree spiking. Some people like to spike the base of each tree, so that the sawyer, in felling the tree, will almost certainly encounter one of the spikes with the chain saw. This would at the very least require the sawyer to stop and sharpen the saw, and might require the replacement of the chain. If this happens with enough trees, the amount of "down time" caused to the sawyers would pose a serious hindrance to operations. In this type of spiking, the spiker drives several nails (or non-metallic spikes . . .) at a downward angle into the first two or three feet above ground of each tree. The nails are spaced so that a sawyer, in felling the tree, is likely to hit at least one of them.

There is an objection to this type of spiking—the possibility, however remote, that the sawyer might be injured, either by the kickback of the saw striking the nail, or by the chain, should it break when striking the spike. A friend of ours who worked for many years as a logger in Colorado says that in numerous incidents of striking metal objects with his saw—including one time when the impact was great enough to cause him to swallow his chaw of tobacco—he never once had a broken chain or was otherwise hurt. Yet the possibility is there. Because of this possibility, we do not recommend this type of spiking.

The second philosophy of tree spiking is to place the spikes in the trees well above the area where the fellers will operate—as many feet up the trunk as one can conveniently work. The object of the spiking in this case is to destroy the blades in the sawmill. . . . Locally owned and operated sawmills are seldom a major threat to wilderness. The major threats come from the big, multinational corporations whose "cut-and-run" philosophy devastates the land and leaves the local economy in shambles when all the big trees are cut and the main office decides to pull out and move to greener pastures.

I anticipate an objection at this point. "Wait a minute," someone says, "if the purpose of spiking trees is to save them from being cut, then what good does it do if the tree wrecks a blade in the mill? It's too late to save the tree, isn't it?" The answer is that the value of spiking is as a long-term deterrent. If enough trees in roadless areas are spiked, eventually the corporate thugs in the timber company boardrooms, along with their corrupt lackeys who wear the uniform of the Forest Service, will realize that timber sales in our few remaining wild areas will be prohibitively expensive. And since profits are the goal, they will begin to think twice before violating the wilderness.

23

BILL McKIBBEN

The End of Nature

1989

Arriving in bookstores right after the warmest year ever recorded, The End of Nature, *by Bill McKibben, reached a public fearful about global warming. As this excerpt shows, McKibben did not allay those fears. Instead, he argued that nature as humans had known it for millions of years no longer existed. Nature, as he understood it, consisted of places untouched and forces unaltered by humans and their technologies. Because human-induced climate change affected every mile of earth, it brought about the "end of nature." Some readers criticized McKibben's narrow definition for the way it appeared to isolate humans from nature—the very thinking that led people to regard environments as consisting of "resources." Yet McKibben's elegant and mournful essay explains both the science and the politics behind global warming and speaks for the anxiety he and many others feel when confronted by the rising power of humans over the planet.*

The idea of nature will not survive the new global pollution—the carbon dioxide and the CFCs[3] and the like. This new rupture with nature is different not only in scope but also in kind. . . . We have changed the

---

[3]Chlorofluorocarbons (CFCs) are nontoxic, nonflammable chemicals used in the manufacture of aerosol sprays, solvents, and refrigerants. They react with ozone molecules (O_3) to reduce the density of the ozone layer that protects the earth from solar radiation.

Bill McKibben, *The End of Nature* (New York: Doubleday, 1989), 58–60, 96–99.

atmosphere, and thus we are changing the weather. By changing the weather, we make every spot on earth man-made and artificial. We have deprived nature of its independence, and that is fatal to its meaning. Nature's independence *is* its meaning; without it there is nothing but us.

If you travel by plane and dog team and snowshoe to the farthest corner of the Arctic and it is a mild summer day, you will not know whether the temperature is what it is "supposed" to be, or whether, thanks to the extra carbon dioxide, you are standing in the equivalent of a heated room. If it is twenty below and the wind is howling— perhaps absent man it would be forty below. Since most of us get to the North Pole only in our minds, the real situation is more like this: if in July there's a heat wave in London, it won't be a natural phenomenon. It will be a man-made phenomenon—an amplification of what nature intended or a total invention. Or, at the very least, it *might* be a man-made phenomenon, which amounts to the same thing. The storm that might have snapped the hot spell may never form, or may veer off in some other direction, not by the laws of nature but by the laws of nature as they have been rewritten, blindly, crudely, but effectively, by man. If the sun is beating down on you, you will not have the comfort of saying, "Well, that's nature." Or if the sun feels sweet on the back of your neck, that's fine, but it isn't nature. A child born now will never know a natural summer, a natural autumn, winter, or spring. Summer is going extinct, replaced by something else that will be called "summer." This new summer will retain some of its relative characteristics—it will be hotter than the rest of the year, for instance, and the time of year when crops grow—but it will not be summer, just as even the best prosthesis is not a leg.

And, of course, climate determines an enormous amount of the rest of nature—where the forests stop and the prairies or the tundra begins, where the rain falls and where the arid deserts squat, where the wind blows strong and steady, where the glaciers form, how fast the lakes evaporate, where the seas rise. As John Hoffman, of the Environmental Protection Agency, noted in the *Journal of Forestry*, "trees planted today will be entering their period of greatest growth when the climate has already changed." A child born today might swim in a stream free of toxic waste, but he won't ever see a natural stream. If the waves crash up against the beach, eroding dunes and destroying homes, it is not the awesome power of Mother Nature. It is the awesome power of Mother Nature as altered by the awesome power of man, who has overpowered in a century the processes that have been slowly evolving and changing of their own accord since the earth was born.

Those "record highs" and "record lows" that the weathermen are always talking about—they're meaningless now. It's like comparing pole vaults between athletes using bamboo and those using fiberglass poles, or dash times between athletes who've been chewing steroids and those who've stuck to Wheaties. They imply a connection between the past and the present which doesn't exist. The comparison is like hanging Rembrandts next to Warhols:[4] we live in a postnatural world. Thoreau once said he could walk for half an hour and come to "some portion of the earth's surface where man does not stand from one year's end to another, and there, consequently, politics are not, for they are but the cigar-smoke of a man." Now you could walk half a year and not reach such a spot. Politics—our particular way of life, our ideas about how we should live—now blows its smoke over every inch of the globe. . . .

We have killed off nature—that world entirely independent of us which was here before we arrived and which encircled and supported our human society. There's still something out there, though; in the place of the old nature rears up a new "nature" of our own devising. It is like the old nature in that it makes its points through what we think of as natural processes (rain, wind, heat), but it offers none of the consolations—the retreat from the human world, the sense of permanence, and even of eternity. Instead, each cubic yard of air, each square foot of soil, is stamped indelibly with our crude imprint, our X. A lot that has been written about the greenhouse effect has stressed the violence of this retuned nature—the withering heat waves, the drought, the sea rising to flood streets. It certainly makes dramatic sense to imagine this break with nature as one of those messy divorces where the ex-husband turns up drunk and waving a gun. But it may, on the other hand, be a nature of longer growing seasons and fewer harsh winters. We don't know, can't know.

Simply because it bears our mark doesn't mean we can control it. This new "nature" may not be predictably violent. It won't be predictably *anything*, and therefore it will take us a very long time to work out our relationship with it, if we ever do. The salient characteristic of this new nature is its unpredictability, just as the salient feature of the old nature was its utter dependability. That may sound strange,

---

[4]Andy Warhol (1928–1987) was an artist whose cool depictions of celebrity and consumerism expressed the sameness and blandness of American life.

for we are used to thinking of the manifestations of nature—rain or sunshine, say—as devious, hard to predict. And over short time spans and for particular places they are; the most cheerful and boisterous weathermen are no more reliable in their forecasts than the cheerful and boisterous sportscasters seated next to them. But on any larger scale nature has been quite constant, and on a global scale it has been a model of reliability. In fact, it has been *the* model of reliability—"as sure as summer follows spring."

Where I live, it is safe to plant tomatoes after June 10, and foolish to plant them before May 20; the last frost is almost sure to fall in those three weeks. In the fall, the first frost nearly always shows up at the beginning of September, and there's a killing freeze by month's end. As a consequence there are no farms nearby. There were once—people tried to grow crops on the land for a generation or so after the initial settlement, but the farms failed, people gave up, and now you come across neat stone walls five miles through the forest from any road. And it's the same in other places; virtually all settlement patterns testify to the dependability of nature. Every year during the late summer, the Nile overflows its banks (or did until the Aswan Dam was built). A pilot knows how the air will behave along his flight path—that a tropical air mass in summer over the American Southeast will breed thunderstorms. ("The details," one meteorologist has said, "are as multifarious as geography itself, but much of it has by now been put into manuals.")

Even extreme events, weather emergencies, have been fairly predictable. Mary Austin, in one of her fine essays on the American desert, wrote that storms "have habits to be learned, appointed paths, seasons, and warnings, and they leave you in no doubt about their performances. One who builds his house on a water scar or the rubble of a steep slope must take his chances." Engineers calculate every drainage and wall for the ability to withstand the "hundred-year storm." Every developer who builds a resort along the coast, every underwriter who insures a ship or a plane, does so with a conscious dependence on the reliability of nature. And even more dependent are those of us who rely *unconsciously* on nature's past performance. The farmer, it is true, has always watched for rain, and sometimes his crops have shriveled. But those of us who do our harvesting at the Price Chopper never doubt that enough rain will fall on enough farms, and it always has.

It is this very predictability that has allowed most of us in the Western world to forget about nature, or to assign it a new role—as a place for withdrawing from the cares of the human world. In some parts of the world, nature has been more capricious, withholding the rain one year or two, pouring it down by the lakeful the next. In these places people think about the weather, about nature, more than we do. But even in Bangladesh people have known that for the most part nature would support them—not richly, but support them.

In this unconscious assumption we mimic animals and plants; as Loren Eiseley[5] says, the "inorganic world could and does really exist in a kind of chaos, but before life can pop forth, even as a flower, or a stick insect, or a beetle, it has to have some kind of unofficial assurance of nature's stability, just as we read that stability in the ripple marks impressed in stone, or the rain-marks on a long-vanished beach, or the eye of a hundred-million-year-old trilobite." Nineteenth-century biologists, he writes, were "amazed" when they discovered these fossils, "but wasps and migratory birds were not. They had an old contract, an old promise . . . that nature, in degree, is steadfast and continuous." And this promise has enabled life to establish itself even in the places we think of as harsh, since they have been harsh in a fairly dependable way. Mary Austin, for instance, writes of the water trails of the desert—paths that lead to the old and trusty springs. "The crested quail that troop in the Ceriso are the happiest frequenters of these paths," she writes. "Great floods pour down the trail with that peculiar melting motion of moving quail, twittering, shoving, and shouldering. They splatter into the shallows, drink daintily, shake out small showers over their perfect coats, and melt away into the scrub, preening and pranking, with soft contented noises." There is change, says Eiseley, but it is change at "the slow pace of inorganic life," and the seasons never "come and go too violently." This is "nature's promise—a guarantee that has not been broken in four billion years that the universe has a queer kind of rationality and expectedness about it."

That promise was long since broken for passenger pigeons,[6] and for the salmon who ran into dams on the ancestral streams, and for peregrine falcons who found their eggshells so weakened by DDT that they couldn't reproduce. But now it is broken for us, too— nature's lifetime warranty has expired.

---

[5]Loren Corey Eiseley (1907–1977) was a writer known for his books and essays on social evolution and the relationship between civilization and nature. See "The Folsom Mystery," *Scientific American*, 167 (December 1942).

[6]The passenger pigeon once existed in North America in astonishing numbers—as many as four billion in 1800. Market hunting reduced its numbers to 250,000 by 1896. It has been extinct since 1914.

5
Acting Locally

24

LADY BIRD JOHNSON
Remarks before the General Session
1965

In 1965, President Lyndon Johnson signed the Beautification Act, stipu-
lating more flowers and street trees, walls to hide junkyards, and fewer
billboards. Most legislation originates with the president or in Congress,
but this bill came from the office of the First Lady, Lady Bird Johnson.
Lady Bird insisted that beauty did not lie in wilderness alone, but also in
common places, and that people's surroundings influenced their feelings
and actions. In this belief, she returned to an older meaning of environ-
ment as a set of influences that shape individuals. Lady Bird loved the
arid West, which is why she made billboards the focus of her campaign.
The Beautification Act eliminated billboards from all federal highways in
rural areas, a policy that changed the experience of driving across the
country.

In the catalogue of ills which afflicts mankind, ugliness and the decay
of our cities and countryside are high on America's agenda.

It seems to me that one of the most pressing challenges for the
individual is the depression and the tension resulting from existence
in a world which is increasingly less pleasing to the eye. Our peace of

Beauty for America, White House Conference on Natural Beauty (Washington, D.C.:
Government Printing Office, 1965), 17–22.

mind, our emotions, our spirit—even our souls—are conditioned by what our eyes see.

Ugliness is bitterness. We are all here to try and change that. This conference is a step towards the solution and I think a great one.

Our immediate problem is: How can one best fight ugliness in a nation such as ours—where there is great freedom of action or inaction for every individual and every interest—where there is virtually no artistic control—and where all action must originate with the single citizen or group of citizens?

That is the immediate problem and challenge. Most of the great cities and great works of beauty of the past were built by autocratic societies. The Caesars built Rome. Paris represents the will of the Kings of France and the Empire. Vienna is the handiwork of the Hapsburgs, and Florence of the Medici.

Can a great democratic society generate the concerted drive to plan, and having planned, to execute great projects of beauty?

I not only hope so—I am certain that it can.

All our national history proves that a committed citizenry is a mighty force when it bends itself to a determined effort. There is a growing feeling in this land today that ugliness has been allowed too long, that it is time to say, "Enough," and to act. . . .

I have heard said—and many times—that among our greatest ills is the deep sense of frustration which the individual feels when he faces the complex and large problems of our century. Ugliness is not that sort of problem. Its vast scope will call for much coordination on the highest levels. But—and this is the blessing of it—it is one problem which every man and woman and child can attack and contribute to defeating. Natural beauty may be a national concern and there is much that government can and should do, but it is the individual who not only benefits, but who must protect a heritage of beauty for future generations.

There are no autocrats in our land to decree beauty, only a national will. Through your work, I firmly believe this national will can be given energy and force, and produce a more beautiful America. . . .

The beauty of our land is a natural resource. Its preservation is linked to the inner prosperity of the human spirit.

The tradition of our past is equal to today's threat to that beauty. Our land will be attractive tomorrow only if we organize for action and rebuild and reclaim the beauty we inherited. Our stewardship will be judged by the foresight with which we carry out these programs. We must rescue our cities and countryside from blight with the same purpose and vigor with which, in other areas, we moved to save the forests and the soil. . . .

There are no panels on such elements of beauty as national parks and forests or wilderness. They are so obviously important that the point need not be belabored. They should have our continuing support, but we believe that this conference should concentrate on new ideas that have not received as much attention as they should.

We have also not specifically included water and air pollution control. Perhaps no problems are more important to the quality of environment and to our general health and well-being, but there are established research and action programs in this field. They need to be improved but we can affirm our strong support for pollution control and move on.

25

BEN H. BAGDIKIAN

The Rape of the Land

1966

The spread of low-density suburban development became an environmental issue because it threatened the open spaces that served as buffers around cities and replaced ecological diversity with monochromatic blandness. Sprawl is more than ugly. It demands federal money for roads, creates the need for more driving and thus more energy, and adds to air pollution. But journalist Ben Bagdikian had other concerns in "The Rape of the Land," an article he wrote for the Saturday Evening Post, *one of the most popular magazines in the United States during the 1960s. He found a longing, a sadness, a sense of loss in suburban development that is well-reflected in the tone of this excerpt. Many of the people he interviewed spoke about the rivers and fields they remembered, now paved over. The article asked a question that forms part of the critique of economic growth offered by environmentalism: Is the American Dream consuming the American landscape?*

Ben H. Bagdikian, "The Rape of the Land," *Saturday Evening Post*, 239 (June 18, 1966): 25–29, 86–94.

All over the United States—in the cities, the suburbs, the country-side, at the seashore—Americans are waking to share the shock and dilemma of . . . the loss of natural open space, which men now realize they need in their neighborhoods to sustain the spirit and relieve the stresses of 20th-century living. . . . As more and more Americans rush to the few remaining convenient open spaces to build their homes or to take vacations, they destroy what they seek.

Is there an answer to this dilemma? The President of the United States thinks there is. President Johnson has proposed, and Congress has already enacted, measures to preserve naturalness where it already exists. He has challenged Congress to help insure that there will be "a patch of sky for every person, a chance to live near an open space and to reach it on a safe street."

Mrs. Johnson, equally concerned, has traveled widely to remind Americans that the beauty of their country is as precious as its coal and iron.

Already the Government has taken some tentative steps. A new Department of Housing and Urban Development is beginning to look at urban life. New programs will try to salvage the best in the American environment. Last year the Federal Government spent $1.3 billion to end pollution of air and water, to study urban chaos and to preserve natural beauty. This is twice its expenditure of five years before. But it is still picayune compared to the vastness of the problem and the speed with which open space is disappearing.

But a start has been made. More than ever before, scholars, scientists and planners are concentrating on the natural and the human environment. The most hopeful sign of all, however, is that this is not a revolution imposed from above but one rising from the bottom. In every city and in thousands of towns and obscure neighborhoods, there are housewives and homeowners banding together to fight, block by block, sometimes tree by tree, to save a small hill, a tiny brook, a stand of maples. The fight to preserve the spectacles of nature—the majestic rivers, the remote mountains, the wild canyons—is 100 years old. The struggle to save the modest beauty of men's own backyards is new and promising.

But it is a confused struggle. It conflicts with men's frantic demands for new homes, broad highways and easy vacations, and with businessmen who are doing what comes naturally to meet these demands. It is even at odds with an old American tradition. For most of our history, space—the unused air, the primitive place, the vast silence—has been considered the enemy. Americans found themselves alone on an immense and wild continent, and progress, to them, meant destroying the wilderness, taming the rivers, filling the landscape with buildings. This idea of progress is deeply imbedded in the American character; even today there is something in us that impels us to vanquish an open place rather than leave it alone.

The mindless destruction of natural places has affected every region of this country.

—In California's Santa Monica Mountains, the wild range that runs from central Los Angeles to the Pacific Ocean, builders have "developed" 70 percent of the slopes, denuding the hills and gashing the terrain with ugly scars. So careless were they about the land that dozens of the new structures, including large apartment houses, have fallen down the mountain.

—In Missouri, St. Louis's most bucolically named road, the Daniel Boone Express Highway, which ran alongside the city's Forest Park, was widened by taking parkland. The highway project paid the park system $858,000 for the acreage it took. To replace those acres the park would have to buy other developed land costing more than two million dollars, which probably means that the city has forever lost precious parkland.

—In Maryland, the town of Greenbelt no longer has its belt of greenery. During the Depression the Federal Government created three such "green belt" communities to act as models. But in the early 1950's, the Government sold all the greenbelt space to private developers, and now the Maryland "model" has lost 70 percent of its green acreage to apartments and shopping centers, with more losses planned.

—In Wisconsin, the second model greenbelt town, Greendale, 10 miles from Milwaukee, has lost its greenbelt in the last 14 years. One thousand acres have already gone to residences, and there is a chance that the remainder may go, too.

—In Ohio, the third model town, Greenhills, 15 miles from Cincinnati, is fighting in the courts to keep green what remains of its greenbelt. Two thirds of its original open space already is covered by real-estate developments.

Despite man's incursions, the American continent in the 1960's is still largely unoccupied, but the open space is not where the people are. Families have crowded into the urban areas and will continue to, for a good reason: It is in and near the city that one finds jobs, good libraries and hospitals, museums and attractive stores. The urban complex remains the basic unit of civilization, where large groups live close enough to interact, to specialize their work, to share their purchasing power and their talent.

In the last generation something has happened that until recently few people understood. In 1910 a majority of Americans still lived in the countryside on farms; most of the 2,300 towns had less than 10,000 population, and were clearly defined units, each separated from other communities by dozens or hundreds of miles of open land and virgin forest. By 1960 most Americans lived in 6,000 urban places, 25 of these over 500,000 in population; these great sprawling masses had begun to touch each other, so that in photographs taken from space there appeared to be continuous stretches of city, like the 500 miles from Chicago to Buffalo, or the 800 miles from Richmond to Bangor. Today, in these vast conglomerations of house, factory, office building, highway and parking lot, ever larger masses of human beings—35 million between Washington and Boston alone—try to live and try to find convenient open, green space.

The crisis is worsening. Each year three million more Americans move into existing cities, the majority to places with populations already greater than 500,000. Fields, woods and hills near urban places are disappearing at the rate of a million acres a year, so that more people find themselves returning home from nervous (rather than physical) work by way of jammed cars, buses and trains to graceless neighborhoods and homes from which they see mostly the walls of surrounding buildings. In desperate need of relief, solitude and beauty, they find themselves among awkward, ugly manmade structures that take a growing toll in bleakness of spirit and mental disease.

There are rational and graceful ways for communities to grow, but as action is delayed, the civilized neighborhoods and the natural places are rapidly disappearing. . . .

The answer seems to lie in the fact that what is often the great advantage of the city—interaction of many people, a large normal intake of sights, sounds, ideas and emotions—can also be an intolerable disadvantage unless the interaction and intake are orderly, with easy and periodic repose and solitude and convenient escape from the cubicles of urban living to the spaciousness and grace of nature.

Cities have grown helter-skelter, usually without much regard for the nervous systems of the human beings who will inhabit them. The greatest shapers of the town have been the price of real estate and the zeal of the highway engineer. There has been a prolonged spasm of uncontrolled building to provide the largest and fastest cash profit; the people who must live in the buildings and neighborhoods are almost an afterthought. Men have drawn lines on maps for highways, usually not knowing that they were doing much more than making a trail for motor vehicles but were in fact destroying old patterns of life and forcing human beings into new and irrational ones.

Building urban America solely for the quick return in the marketplace has taken a frightful toll in social and individual stress. The rich, fleeing dehumanized central cities, have gone to the suburbs, where they have discovered that the greenery and space they were looking for is like the horizon—the more you reach out for it, the farther away it gets. In a few years the new suburbs became as barren as downtown streets.

The disorderly sprawl of cities is expensive. For every $20,000 suburban house sold, it costs the municipality $18,000 in services like sewers and schools, plus $1,000 a year in upkeep. The hidden physical costs make the bill even higher. Quick and careless scraping of the earth for highways and housing removes green cover, leaving exposed scars. The result is flooding and sedimentation damage of one billion dollars a year. This is what colors most American rivers brown. . . .

Some argue that the preservation of natural space within an urban setting is profitable in dollars and cents because it increases the tax value of the surrounding property.

But the ultimate purpose is to enrich not the bank account but the human spirit. This notion was forcefully expressed not long ago by a man who looked unlikely to deliver a defense of beauty for its own sake. He is a retired naval captain with close-cropped hair, a stiff back and eyes like frozen grapes.

"If you identify me I'll call you a liar," he said, "because it will wipe me out with the town council. I'm on the council and I'm fighting to keep the pond up on the hill by the poplar trees. The reason I want to keep that pond is aesthetics, pure and simple. Yes, aesthetics. They think that's a fancy word. I just think it's a beautiful place. My wife and I used to go up there and I used to take my son there when he was a kid to watch the swallows skimming over the water and listen to the evening wind going through those poplars. I happen to think that's worth a hell of a lot to this community. Now my son comes back here and he takes his son up there.

"You know what the councilmen want to do with it? Let a guy put up a motel. You know what that guy is going to do? He's going to cut

down all the poplars and bulldoze the pond full of dirt. Hell, he can do
that down by the highway. They want to give him his permit but I'm
fighting. Do I dare to talk to them about aesthetics? Hell, no! I'm
giving them the damnedest argument you ever heard in the only language they respect—dollars and cents. I've almost got them convinced they'll show a profit by turning this landscape wrecker down.
But the real reason is aesthetics. It's a beautiful place. Why can't an
American town be beautiful?"

26

Santa Barbara Declaration of Environmental Rights

1970

*On January 28, 1969, workers on Union Oil's Platform A, a tower off
the coast of California used to extract petroleum from the ocean floor, discovered one of their drilling tubes stuck in a well. When they pulled it
out, five gashes opened in the ocean floor. During the next hundred days,
more than 200,000 gallons of crude oil washed up on a thirty-mile shore-
line centered on the city of Santa Barbara. The spill quickly transformed
from a local story to a national story. A gripping photo of an oil-soaked
bird appeared on the cover of* National Geographic. *New environmental
action groups, including Greenpeace and Pollution Probe, formed in
direct response. The California State Land Commission banned off-shore
oil drilling for sixteen years. This declaration was issued by a group of
citizens who thought beyond sullied beaches to larger questions—what
they called a "revolution in conduct."*

All men have the right to an environment capable of sustaining life
and promoting happiness. If the accumulated actions of the past
become destructive of this right, men now living have the further
right to repudiate the past for the benefit of the future. And it is mani-

Congressional Record, 91st Cong., 2nd sess., January 20, 1970.

fest that centuries of careless neglect of the environment have brought mankind to a final crossroads. The quality of our lives is eroded and our very existence threatened by our abuse of the natural world.

Moved by an environmental disaster in the Santa Barbara Channel to think and act in national and world terms, we submit these charges:

We have littered the land with refuse.

We have encroached upon our heritage of open space and wild-land.

We have stripped the forests and the grasses and reduced the soil to fruitless dust.

We have contaminated the air we breathe for life.

We have befouled the lakes and rivers and oceans along with their shorelines.

We have released deadly poisons into earth, air, and water, imperiling all life.

We have exterminated entire species of birds and animals and brought others close to annihilation.

We are overpopulating the earth.

We have made much of the physical work ugly and loud, depriving man of the beauty and quiet that feeds his spirit.

Recognizing that the ultimate remedy for these fundamental problems is found in man's mind, not his machines, we call on societies and their governments to recognize and implement the following principles:

We need an ecological consciousness that recognizes man as member, not master, of the community of living things sharing his environment.

We must extend ethics beyond social relations to govern man's contact with all life forms and with the environment itself.

We need a renewed idea of community, which will shape urban environments that serve the full range of human needs.

We must find the courage to take upon ourselves as individuals the responsibility for the welfare of the whole environment, treating our own back yards as if they were the world and the world as if it were our back yard.

We must develop the vision to see that in regard to the natural world private and corporate ownership should be so limited as to preserve the interest of society and the integrity of the environment.

We need greater awareness of our enormous powers on the
fragility of the earth, and the consequent responsibility of
men and governments for its preservation.
We must redefine "progress" toward an emphasis on long-term
quality rather than immediate quantity.

We therefore, resolve to act. We propose a revolution in conduct
toward an environment which is rising in revolt against us. Granted
that ideas and institutions long established are not easily changed; yet
today is the first day of the rest of our life on this planet. We will begin
anew.

27

WENDELL BERRY

The Agricultural Crisis as a Crisis of Culture
1977

*Agrarians believe that industrial capitalism has eroded the relationship
between humans and the land that feeds and clothes them. Agrarian
thought is suffused with an ethic of consumption that is close kin to environmentalism, but long predates it. According to agrarians, the moral
quality of a crop depends on the integrity of the environment that produced it. Many of the people who read the* Whole Earth Catalog *and
joined back-to-the-land communities formed an audience receptive to
agrarian critiques of American society. By the late 1970s, they were
reading Wendell Berry, a farmer, essayist, and poet who lives in Henry
County, Kentucky. As seen in this excerpt from* The Unsettling of America, *Berry directed his fury at the state of agriculture in America, especially the shift in scale and purpose he saw in mechanized farms
supported by university experiment stations. Berry's insight is that distinctive landscapes are preserved by distinct social identities.*

Wendell Berry, *The Unsettling of America: Culture and Agriculture* (San Francisco:
Sierra Club Books, 1977), 41–48.

Along with the rest of society, the established agriculture has shifted its emphasis, and its interest, from quality to quantity, having failed to see that in the long run the two ideas are inseparable. To pursue quantity alone is to destroy those disciplines in the producer that are the only assurance of quantity. What is the effect on quantity of persuading a producer to produce an inferior product? What, in other words, is the relation of pride or craftsmanship to abundance? That is another question the "agribusinessmen" and their academic collaborators do not ask. They do not ask it because they are afraid of the answer: The preserver of abundance is excellence.

My point is that food is a cultural product; it cannot be produced by technology alone. Those agriculturists who think of the problems of food production solely in terms of technological innovation are over-simplifying both the practicalities of production and the network of meanings and values necessary to define, nurture, and preserve the practical motivations. That the discipline of agriculture should have been so divorced from other disciplines has its immediate cause in the compartmental structure of the universities, in which complementary, mutually sustaining and enriching disciplines are divided, according to "professions," into fragmented, one-eyed specialties. . . .

However, if we conceive of a culture as one body, which it is, we see that all of its disciplines are everybody's business, and that the proper university product is therefore not the whittled-down, isolated mentality of expertise, but a mind competent in all its concerns. To such a mind it would be clear that there are agricultural disciplines that have nothing to do with crop production, just as there are agricultural obligations that belong to people who are not farmers.

A culture is not a collection of relics or ornaments, but a practical necessity, and its corruption invokes calamity. A healthy culture is a communal order of memory, insight, value, work, conviviality, reverence, aspiration. It reveals the human necessities and the human limits. It clarifies our inescapable bonds to the earth and to each other. It assures that the necessary restraints are observed, that the necessary work is done, and that it is done well. A healthy *farm* culture can be based only upon familiarity and can grow only among a people soundly established upon the land; it nourishes and safeguards a human intelligence of the earth that no amount of technology can satisfactorily replace. The growth of such a culture was once a strong possibility in the farm communities of this country. We now have only the sad remnants of those communities. If we allow another generation to pass without doing what is necessary to enhance and embolden the possibility now perishing with them, we will lose it altogether. And then we will not only invoke calamity—we will deserve it. . . .

The concentration of the farmland into larger and larger holdings and fewer and fewer hands—with the consequent increase of overhead, debt, and dependence on machines—is thus a matter of complex significance, and its agricultural significance cannot be disentangled from its cultural significance. It *forces* a profound revolution in the farmer's mind: once his investment in land and machines is large enough, he must forsake the values of husbandry and assume those of finance and technology. Thenceforth his thinking is not determined by agricultural responsibility, but by financial accountability and the capacities of his machines. Where his money comes from becomes less important to him than where it is going. He is caught up in the drift of energy and interest away from the land. Production begins to override maintenance. The economy of money has infiltrated and subverted the economies of nature, energy, and the human spirit. The man himself has become a consumptive machine.

For some time now ecologists have been documenting the principle that "you can't do one thing"—which means that in a natural system whatever affects one thing ultimately affects everything. Everything in the Creation is related to everything else and dependent on everything else. The Creation is one; it is a uni-verse, a whole, the parts of which are all "turned into one."

A good agricultural system, which is to say a durable one, is similarly unified. In the 1940s, the great British agricultural scientist, Sir Albert Howard, published *An Agricultural Testament* and *The Soil and Health*, in which he argued against the influence in agriculture of "the laboratory hermit" who had substituted "that dreary principle [official organization] for the soul-shaking principle of that essential freedom needed by the seeker after truth." And Howard goes on to speak of the disruptiveness of official organization: "The natural universe, which is one, has been halved, quartered, fractioned. . . . Real organization always involves real responsibility: the official organization of research tries to retain power and avoid responsibility by sheltering behind groups of experts." Howard himself began as a laboratory hermit: "I could not take my own advice before offering it to other people." But he saw the significance of the "wide chasm between science in the laboratory and practice in the field." He devoted his life to bridging that chasm. His is the story of a fragmentary intelligence seeking both its own wholeness and that of the world. The aim that he finally realized in his books was to prepare the way "for treating the whole problem of health in soil, plant, animal, and man as one great subject." He unspecialized his vision, in other words, so as to see the necessary unity of the concerns of agriculture, as well as the convergence of these concerns with concerns of other kinds: biological, historical, medical, moral, and so on. He sought to establish agriculture upon the same unifying cycle that preserves health, fertility, and renewal in nature: the Wheel of Life (as he called it, borrowing the term from religion), by which "Death supersedes life and life rises again from what is dead and decayed."

It remains only to say what has often been said before—that the best human cultures also have this unity. Their concerns and enterprises are not fragmented, scattered out, at variance or in contention with one another. The people and their work and their country are members of each other and of the culture. If a culture is to hope for any considerable longevity, then the relationships within it must, in recognition of their interdependence, be predominantly cooperative rather than competitive. A people cannot live long at each other's expense or at the expense of their cultural birthright—just as an agriculture cannot live long at the expense of its soil or its work force, and just as in a natural system the competitions among species must be limited if all are to survive.

In any of these systems, cultural or agricultural or natural, when a species or group exceeds the principle of usufruct (literally, the "use of the fruit"), it puts itself in danger. Then, to use an economic metaphor, it is living off the principal rather than the interest. It has broken out of the system of nurture and has become exploitive; it is destroying what gave it life and what it depends upon to live. In all of these systems a fundamental principle must be the protection of the source: the seed, the food species, the soil, the breeding stock, the old and the wise, the keepers of memories, the records.

And just as competition must be strictly curbed within these systems, it must be strictly curbed *among* them. An agriculture cannot survive long at the expense of the natural systems that support it and that provide it with models. A culture cannot survive long at the expense either of its agricultural or of its natural sources. To live at the expense of the source of life is obviously suicidal. Though we have no choice but to live at the expense of other life, it is necessary to ʳ ognize the limits and dangers involved: past a certain point in a ʸ system, "other life" is our own.

The definitive relationships in the universe are thus noᵗ but interdependent. And from a human point of view tʰ cal. We can build one system only within another. Wᵛ ture only within nature, and culture only within ag critical points these systems have to conform with one another or destroy one another.

Under the discipline of unity, knowledge and morality come together. No longer can we have that paltry "objective" knowledge so prized by the academic specialists. To know anything at all becomes a moral predicament. Aware that there is no such thing as a specialized—or even an entirely limitable or controllable—effect, one becomes responsible for judgments as well as facts. Aware that as an agricultural scientist he had "one great subject," Sir Albert Howard could no longer ask, What can I do with what I know? without at the same time asking, How can I be responsible for what I know?

And it is within unity that we see the hideousness and destructiveness of the fragmentary—the kind of mind, for example, that can introduce a production machine to increase "efficiency" without troubling about its effect on workers, on the product, and on consumers; that can accept and even applaud the "obsolescence" of the small farm and not hesitate over the possible political and cultural effects; that can recommend continuous tillage of huge monocultures, with massive use of chemicals and no animal manure or humus, and worry not at all about the deterioration or loss of soil. For cultural patterns of responsible cooperation we have substituted this moral ignorance, which is the etiquette of agricultural "progress."

28

LOIS GIBBS

Knocking on Doors at Love Canal
1983

The trauma over the toxic chemicals buried under her neighborhood of Love Canal, New York, transformed Lois Gibbs into a grassroots activist for health and safety. In 1983, she reflected on her coming of age, after having gained national attention and even having influenced the first federal law for cleaning up toxic waste (the Superfund Law) without the

---

`bs, *Love Canal: My Story* (Albany: State University of New York Press, 1983),
`3.

*aid of any of the major environmental organizations—none of which
had ever pursued the problem of toxic waste before. In this excerpt from
her autobiography, Gibbs and a few of her neighbors knock on doors to
gain support, travel to the state capitol at Albany for a meeting with
health officials, and end up at a street rally back at home, in which
Gibbs is thrust before a microphone for the first time.*

It was terribly warm and humid that day. The closer I got to the canal,
the more I could smell it. I could *feel* it, too, it was so humid. The odor
seemed to hang in the thick air. My nose began to run, and my eyes
were watering. I thought it was psychosomatic. I hadn't been eating
properly and I was tired. Maybe, I thought, I'm just oversensitive. But my
consciousness of the danger of the chemicals was not yet roused. . . .

As I proceeded down 99th Street, I developed a set speech. I would
tell people what I wanted. But the speech wasn't all that necessary. It
seemed as though every home on 99th Street had someone with an illness. One family had a young daughter with arthritis. They couldn't
understand why she had it at her age. Another daughter had had a
miscarriage. The father, still a fairly young man, had had a heart
attack. I went to the next house, and there, people would tell me *their*
troubles. People were reaching out; they were telling me their
troubles in hopes I would do something. But I didn't know anything to
do. I was also confused. I just wanted to stop children from going to
that school. Now look at all those other health problems! Maybe they
were related to the canal. But even if they were, what could I do?

As I continued going door-to-door, I heard more. The more I heard,
the more frightened I became. This problem involved much more
than the 99th Street School. The entire community seemed to be sick!
Then I remembered my own neighbors. One who lived on the left of
my husband and me was suffering from severe migraines and had
been hospitalized three or four times that year. Her daughter had kid-
ney problems and bleeding. A woman on the other side of us had gas-
trointestinal problems. A man in the next house down was dying of
lung cancer and he didn't even work in industry. The man across the
street had just had lung surgery. . . . [M]aybe there *was* more to it
than just the school. I didn't understand how chemicals could get all
the way over to 101st Street from 99th; but the more I thought about
it, the more frightened I became—for my family and for the whole
neighborhood. . . .

I continued to go door-to-door. I was becoming more worried because of the many families with children who had birth defects. Then I learned something even more frightening: there had been five crib deaths within a few short blocks. . . .

We stopped at every rest stop on the way to Albany. . . . When we got to Albany, we were flabbergasted. None of us had ever been there before. We didn't know where we were. We wanted to find the South Mall Campus, where the state government buildings are concentrated. When we had located it, we would find a hotel. That way, it would be easy to get to the meeting the next morning. . . .

The following morning we drove to the mall. In the daylight, it seemed even more incredible. It's immense. Inside, it looks like a spaceship. The corridors made us feel as if we were in a huge cement-and-tile maze.

We went to Dr. David Axelrod's office, where we were told the meeting would be downstairs in a larger room because of the 161 Love Canal residents who were expected. We had brought a petition with 161 *names* on it; there was no need for the big conference room. The lady from 97th Street was already in the room. She didn't seem happy to see us though. By concidence, she and I were wearing identical shirts!

Commissioner Robert Whalen, Dr. Vianna, Dr. Axelrod (who would become the next health commissioner), Dr. Kim, and a few others were sitting on the stage. Commissioner Whalen stood up and began the meeting. He read an order stating that the residents of Love Canal were not to eat food from their gardens and that the 99th Street School would be closed during remedial construction. The bombshell came when he recommended the evacuation of pregnant women and children under the age [of] two because, he said, the state was concerned about a danger to their health. Whalen backed up this statement with data and statistics. He didn't say the state *would* move all those people, just that they *should* move. The state order stipulated only pregnant women and children under the age of two. What, I wondered, were the rest of their families supposed to do—leave them there?

With that I almost lost my cool. Then I remembered what Wayne had said about the press and the first fifteen minutes. Still, I was furious. I jumped up and said to Commissioner Whalen: "If the dump will hurt pregnant women and children under two, what for God's sake, is it going to do to the rest of us!? What do you think you're doing?" Now very emotional, I said; "You can't do that! That would be murder!"

Debbie joined in: "Wait a minute, wait a minute. My kids are *over* two. Are you trying to tell me my children are safe?" (Debbie's backyard was right on the canal. If the commissioner had made his decision two months earlier, he would have moved her, but not now.) Between the two of us, we kept the meeting in an uproar for some fifteen minutes. "We can't eat out of our garden. We can't go in our backyard. We can't have children under two. We can't be pregnant. You're telling us it's safe for the rest of us!"

Commissioner Whalen left for a ten-minute break. He said he would come back, but he didn't, and that made me angry all over again. In the meantime, I talked to Dr. Vianna. He walked up and down, up and down, insisting that he couldn't find any problem. There just wasn't that much abnormality. I told him I thought he was dead wrong. I had learned about five crib deaths myself, just by walking around, and I wasn't doing a health survey. Many women told me they had miscarried. I found sick people all around the canal. "You can't stand there and tell me there's no problem at Love Canal!" According to his survey, he didn't see any. I kept telling him the survey must not have been conducted properly. I told him about the five crib deaths, that most of those women had been breast-feeding. Dr. Vianna kept pacing. "You'll just have to get the residents to fill out health forms and sign them," he said. "You'll have to push the residents if you want to get anything done." In his own way, he was trying to be helpful; at the same time, he wasn't giving us any assurances.

When the meeting reconvened, Frank Rovers of Conestoga Rovers[1] was on the stage to explain the remedial construction plan. He was the engineer who had drawn it up. I was still boiling from my talk with Dr. Vianna, and I now attacked Rovers. "Wait a minute," I said; "What about the underground streams?" He said they would be taken care of and gave me a technical explanation I didn't understand. "Excuse me," I replied. "I'm just a dumb housewife. I'm not an expert. *You're* the expert. I'm just going to use a little common sense. You will have underground streams running through the canal beneath those pipelines. The chemicals will get out. There's no way they are going to go into your pipe. They will be *under* it. Now, how do you *take care* of that?" He answered with some more incomprehensible engineering terms. . . .

---

[1]Conestoga Rovers and Associates was the engineering firm hired by the State of New York to address the chemicals in Love Canal.

When we got back to Niagara Falls, we drove to my house to see the kids. My mother was standing on the sidewalk, waving both arms. "Get right over to 99th Street," she yelled. "They're having a street meeting. They've all gone crazy." I thought my *mother* had gone crazy, standing there in the middle of the street yelling at me. I was exhausted. We had had two or three hours sleep, and we had been driving much of the day. . . .

Hundreds of people were in the street, screaming, yelling, and talking—and burning papers in a bucket. I had never seen anything like it. They were like a mob, feelings were running so high. When I saw Wayne and Kathy, I got out of the car.

Tom Heisner was standing on a box, holding a microphone. "Is Lois Gibbs back from Albany yet? Is Lois Gibbs back from Albany?" I walked around hoping no one would notice me. Wayne and Kathy said they had heard about the health commissioner's statement on the radio. "It's wild. There's no one here from the health department, or any department, to explain what it means." Just then somebody in the crowd recognized me and pushed me up to the microphone.

I had never spoken to a group of people in my whole life. In high school, if I had to do a book report in front of the class, I would cut the class. It just wasn't my way. Nevertheless, I introduced myself to Tom and Lois Heisner. Tom Heisner was telling people to burn their mortgages, to tear up their tax bills. "We're not paying anything. This house is worthless, useless. It's not worth anything. It's no good. It's uninhabitable. We can't live here." And a lot of residents were doing it. They were bringing up papers and putting them in a bucket to be burned.

I was nervous. I had a habit of saying "OK" after everything I said. I would say "OK? I'd like to talk to you, OK? I'd like to talk to you about something that is going on, OK?" It was a speech habit, or maybe I had so little confidence in myself that I was asking people for permission to speak. Wayne took it upon himself to cure my habit by sticking his finger up every time I said OK—to make me conscious of what I was saying. Wayne sensed I could become a leader; in his own way, he was trying to train me.

I got up to the microphone and stood there looking out at about 400 people. Some were pregnant women, some little children, some senior citizens; there were people of all ages, colors, sexes, and sizes. Tom Heisner introduced me. All those faces were looking up, waiting for me to say something.

29

CÉSAR CHÁVEZ

What Is the Worth of a Man or a Woman?

1989

For decades, the major environmental organizations paid no attention to the unequal working and living conditions of the poor and politically powerless. Environmental justice became part of the larger movement in a very different way than wilderness—by provoking outrage. Farm workers who harvested grapes in the San Joaquin Valley of California lived in shanties and endured pesticide applications where they worked and slept. In 1965, César Chávez, born in 1927 into a family of farm laborers, began to publicize a boycott of table grapes in order to compel grape growers to improve the housing of farm laborers. News of Chávez and the appalling poverty of the people he represented reached Senator Robert Kennedy, who marched with Chávez and endorsed the United Farm Workers. Chávez expanded the political boundaries of environmentalism to include the safety and dignity of some of the poorest people in the United States.

What is the worth of a man or a woman? What is the worth of a farm worker? How do you measure the value of a life?

Ask the parents of Johnnie Rodriguez. Johnnie Rodriguez was not even a man; Johnnie was a five year old boy when he died after a painful two year battle against cancer.

His parents, Juan and Elia, are farm workers. Like all grape workers, they are exposed to pesticides and other agricultural chemicals. Elia worked in the table grapes around Delano, California until she was eight months pregnant with Johnnie. Juan and Elia cannot say for certain if pesticides caused their son's cancer. But neuroblastoma is one of the cancers found in McFarland, a small farm town only a few miles from Delano, where the Rodriguezes live.

Address by César Chávez, Pacific Lutheran University, Tacoma, Wash., March 1989 (The César E. Chávez Foundation).

"Pesticides are always in the fields and around the towns," Johnnie's father told us. "The children get the chemicals when they play outside, drink the water or when they hug you after you come home from working in fields that are sprayed."

"Once your son has cancer, it's pretty hard to take," Juan Rodriguez says. "You hope it's a mistake, you pray. He was a real nice boy. He took it strong and lived as long as he could."

I keep a picture of Johnnie Rodriguez. He is sitting on his bed, hugging his Teddy bears. His sad eyes and cherubic face stare out at you. The photo was taken four days before he died.

Johnnie Rodriguez was one of 13 McFarland children diagnosed with cancer in recent years; and one of six who have died from the disease. With only 6,000 residents, the rate of cancer in McFarland is 400 percent above normal. In McFarland and in Fowler childhood cancer cases are being reported in excess of expected rates. In Delano and other farming towns, questions are also being raised.

The chief source of carcinogens in these communities are pesticides from the vineyards and fields that encircle them. Health experts believe the high rate of cancer in McFarland is from pesticides and nitrate-containing fertilizers leaching into the water system from surrounding fields. . . .

Our critics sometimes ask, "Why should the United Farm Workers worry about pesticides when farm workers have so many other more obvious problems?"

The wealth and plenty of California agribusiness are built atop the suffering of generations of California farm workers. Farm labor history across America is one shameful tale after another of hardship and exploitation. Malnutrition among migrant children. Tuberculosis, pneumonia and respiratory infections. Average life expectancy more than twenty years below the U.S. norm. Savage living conditions. Miserable wages and working conditions. Sexual harassment of women workers. Widespread child labor. Inferior schools or no school at all. . . .

There is nothing we care more about than the lives and safety of our families. There is nothing we share more deeply in common with the consumers of North America than the safety of the food all of us reply upon.

We are proud to be a part of the House of Labor.

Collective bargaining is the traditional way American workers have escaped poverty and improved their standard of living. It is the way farm workers will also empower themselves. But the U.F.W. has always had to be something more than a union. Because our people are so poor. Because the color of our skin is dark. Because we often don't speak the language. Because the discrimination, the racism and the social dilemmas we confront transcend mere economic need.

What good does it do to achieve the blessings of collective bargaining and make economic progress for people when their health is destroyed in the process? If we ignored pesticide poisoning—if we looked on as farm workers and their children are stricken—then all the other injustices our people face would be compounded by an even more deadly tyranny.

But ignore that final injustice is what our opponents would have us do.

"Don't worry," the growers say.

"The U.F.W. misleads the public about dangers pesticides pose to farm workers," the Table Grape Commission says. "Governor Deukmejian's pesticide safety system protects workers," the Farm Bureau proclaims.

Ask the family of Juan Chabolla. Juan Chabolla collapsed after working in a field sprayed only an hour before with Monitor, a deadly pesticide. But instead of rushing Juan to a nearby hospital, the grower drove him 45 miles across the U.S.-Mexico border and left him in a Tijuana clinic. He was dead on arrival.

Juan, 32, left his wife and four young children in their impoverished clapboard shack in Maneadero, Mexico.

Just after Juan Chabolla died, Governor Deukmejian vetoed a modest bill, strongly opposed by agribusiness, that would have required growers to post warning signs in fields where dangerous pesticides are applied.

One billion pounds of pesticides are applied each year in the United States—79 percent of them in agriculture; 250 million pounds go on crops in California; in 1986, 10 million pounds went on grapes. And that 10 million pounds on grapes only covers restricted use pesticides, where permits are required and use is reported. Many other potentially dangerous chemicals are used that don't have to be disclosed.

Grapes is the largest fruit crop in California. It receives more restricted use pesticides than any fresh food crop. About one-third of grape pesticides are known carcinogens—like the chemicals that may have afflicted Johnnie Rodriguez; others are teratogens—birth defect-producing pesticides. . . . Pesticides cause acute poisoning—of the kind that killed Juan Chabolla—and chronic, long-term effects such as we're seeing in communities like McFarland.

More than half of all acute pesticide-related illnesses reported in California involve grape production. In 1987 and '88, entire crews of grape workers—hundreds of people—were poisoned after entering vineyards containing toxic residues. In all those episodes, the grapes had been sprayed weeks before. All the legal requirements were followed. The vineyards were thought to be "safe."

But farm workers were still poisoned. . . .

Farm workers and their families are exposed to pesticides from the crops they work. The soil the crops are grown in. Drift from sprays applied to adjoining fields—and often to the very field where they are working. The fields that surround their homes are heavily and repeatedly sprayed. Pesticides pollute irrigation water and groundwater.

Children are still a big part of the labor force. Or they are taken to the fields by their parents because there is no child care. Pregnant women labor in the fields to help support their families. Toxic exposure begins at a very young age—often in the womb.

What does acute pesticide poisoning produce? Eye and respiratory irritations. Skin rashes. Systemic poisoning.

Death.

What are the chronic effects of pesticide poisoning on people, including farm workers and their children, according to scientific studies? Birth defects. Sterility. Still births. Miscarriages. Neurological and neuropsychological effects. Effects on child growth and development.

Cancer. . . .

You can't fool Mother Nature. Insects can outfox anything we throw at them. In time, they will overcome. People thought pesticides were the cure-all—the key to an abundance of food. They thought pesticides were the solution; but they were the problem.

The problem is this mammoth agribusiness system. The problem are the huge farms. The problem is the pressure on the land from developers. The problem is not allowing the land to lay fallow and recover. The problem is the abandonment of cultural practices that have stood the test of centuries: crop rotation, diversification of crops. The problem is monoculture—growing acres and acres of the same crop; disrupting the natural order of things; letting insects feast on acres and acres of a harem of delight . . . and using pesticides that kill off their natural predators.

Meantime, these greedy chemical companies, multi-national corporations, try to sanctify their poisons. They would have us believe they are the health givers—that because of them people are not dying of malaria and starvation. When all the time, they just want to defend their investments. They just want to protect their profits. They don't want anything to change.

The chemical companies believe in the Domino Theory: if any chemical is attacked then all chemicals are threatened. No matter how dangerous it is.

It's a lot like that saying from the Vietnam War: we had to destroy the village in order to save it.

They have to poison us in order to save us. But at what cost? The lives of farm workers and their children who are suffering? The lives of consumers who could reap the harvest of pesticides ten, twenty years from now? The contamination of our ground water. The loss of our reverence for the soil. The raping of the land.

30

VERNICE D. MILLER

The Quest for Environmental Justice

1993

Vernice D. Miller, cofounder of West Harlem Environmental Action, calls for an integrated response to environmental inequality, including lobbying at the federal level combined with local political involvement. This excerpt is an exemplary document for the fusion between civil rights strategies and environmentalist goals, a connection that will increasingly define the movement in the twenty-first century. Miller argues for the inner city as the locus for a new environmental movement, in which economic equality and environmental quality cannot be separated.

Over the last decade, communities of color across the United States have become aware of a new menace threatening our communities: the siting of environmentally hazardous facilities or substances in the midst of where we live. We want to stop the poisoning of our people

From Richard Hofrichter, ed., *Toxic Struggles: The Theory and Practice of Environmental Justice* (Philadelphia: New Society Publishers, 1993), 129–35.

and of our land. By linking environmental issues to social, racial, and economic justice, we have created a new and dynamic social-justice movement. The environmental-justice movement seeks to change forever the material conditions of people of color in the United States, as well as those whose lives are affected by U.S. policies throughout the world. Ultimately what we seek is a fundamental transformation of society where racial and economic justice prevail.

In 1987, the United Church of Christ Commission for Racial Justice published the landmark study *Toxic Wastes and Race*, which documented and quantified the phenomenon of "environmental racism." The study's findings "suggest the existence of clear patterns which show that communities with greater minority percentages of the population are more likely to be the sites of commercial hazardous waste facilities. The possibility that these patterns resulted by chance is virtually impossible, strongly suggesting that some underlying factors, which are related to race, played a role in the location of commercial hazardous waste facilities. Therefore the Commission for Racial Justice concludes that, indeed, race has been a factor in the location of hazardous waste facilities in the United States."

As a research assistant working on the study, I remember feeling that, finally, somebody understood and believed what we in West Harlem had been saying since 1968—that our community was being used as a dump site for the City of New York primarily because its inhabitants were African American and Latino American.

Since 1987, communities of color across the United States have broadened the context of their struggles for justice to include environmental justice. Many communities that had been engaged in these struggles for some time have redefined their battle, as environmental justice has come to symbolize every aspect of the discriminatory and unequal treatment that we have been experiencing all along.

In every state, some community is organizing and fighting back against the evils of racial discrimination, poverty, and economic and environmental exploitation. The reverberations from these communities have reached a fevered pitch as the environmental-justice movement advances nationally.

The First National People of Color Environmental Leadership Summit

In October 1991, under the sponsorship of the United Church of Christ Commission for Racial Justice, the First National People of Color Environmental Leadership Summit was held in Washington, D.C. According to a paper produced for the Summit, "environmental inequities cannot be reduced solely to class—the economic ability of people to 'vote with their feet' and escape polluted environments. Race interpenetrates class in the United States and is often a more potent predictor of which communities get dumped on and which ones are spared. There is clear evidence that institutional barriers severely limit access to clean environments. Despite the many attempts made by government to level the playing field, all communities are still not equal."

As described by Reverend Ben Chavis in the preface to the proceedings of the Summit, "the Leadership Summit is not an independent 'event' but a significant and pivotal step in the crucial process whereby people of color are organizing themselves and their communities for self-determination and self-empowerment around the central issues of environmental justice. It is living testimony that no longer shall we allow others to define our peoples' future. The very survival of all communities is at stake."

The Summit was a momentous event in the life of the environmental-justice movement. Standing together during the first two days of the Summit, we who had been selected as delegates were reinforced by the multicolored faces of three hundred people who each understood and shared a common commitment to the preservation of all our communities. During the opening session you could see a sea of bobbing heads as the delegates eagerly surveyed the large ballroom where we were all gathered. You could sense what we were all thinking: We're not alone anymore!

For three and a half days we as delegates, later joined by a group of three hundred or so participants and observers, struggled through many difficult moments. We had a very tense session with leaders from mainstream environmental organizations, and many emotional accounts of the real conditions faced by different communities. The conference produced several exercises in democratic process and collective decision making, as well as cross-cultural and group dynamics. . . .

Overall Objectives

The delegates at the Leadership Summit took great pains to draft and ratify the "Principles of Environmental Justice" and affirm the "Call to Action," since both of these documents articulate exactly what we mean when we say we want to transform society. Principles 1 and 5 perhaps best encapsulate the spirit of this movement: "Environmental justice affirms the sacredness of Mother Earth, ecological unity and the interdependence of all species, and the right to be free from ecological destruction," and "Environmental justice affirms the fundamental right to political, economic, cultural and environmental self-determination of all peoples."

As a result of the Summit, and efforts prior to the Summit, several objectives have been set forth for the movement as a whole regarding issues of environmental equity. "[E]nvironmental equity falls into three major categories: *Procedural Equity*, [which] deals with the 'fairness' question, and the extent that governing rules, regulations, and evaluation criteria are applied uniformly across the board. *Geographic Equity*, [which] deals with the idea that some neighborhoods, communities, and regions are disproportionately burdened by hazardous waste. *Social Equity*, [which] deals with the role of race, class, and other cultural factors in environmental decision-making."

The Summit workshops, and significant regional and national follow-up to the Summit objectives, have led this movement to address various equity questions through the following initiatives:

1. to influence and redefine federal legislation and policy-making regarding hazardous-waste production, disposal, and clean-up, and waste-facilities siting;

2. to challenge and eradicate unequal environmental protection by the EPA and other federal agencies, such as the Department of Energy, the U.S. Department of Defense, and the Nuclear Regulatory Commission;

3. to work with academics of color to conduct research that supports local community struggles;

4. to gain control of local political processes, and establish community control of local decision-making processes;

5. to elect or appoint "true" community representatives to decision-making bodies; and, most important,

6. to represent ourselves and speak for ourselves at the tables of power and authority and policy-making.

Plan of Action

... Many exciting developments are occurring nationally, as the environmental-justice movement broadens its focus to address the overarching political and legal framework that undergirds the phenomenon of environmental racism. A group of grass-roots activists, academics, national civil-rights organizations, tribal leaders, and environmental policy experts, all people of color, have been meeting with EPA officials and staff on a regular basis to advise them on policy vis-à-vis environmental-justice issues. Subsequently the EPA has formed a national environmental-equity interagency working group, and has initiated environmental equity projects in three EPA regions across the country. While this is a step forward for EPA, it is, nevertheless, a woefully inadequate response to the catastrophic environmental conditions that many communities of color face.

At this writing the reauthorization of the Resource Recovery Conservation Act (1992) and the Superfund Reauthorization Act (1993) have both had sustained involvement from representatives of the environmental-justice movement, and from members of the Congressional Black Caucus and their staff, in the redrafting of these two significant pieces of federal legislation to more accurately reflect the legislative needs of grass-roots communities. Also in 1992, then-Senator Albert Gore and Congressman John Lewis, in association with Reverend Ben Chavis, introduced the Environmental Justice Act. This legislation is a good start, but grass-roots activists believe that it still misses the mark and is not the type of comprehensive legislation that will help us put an end to the dumping of hazardous wastes and the siting of waste facilities in our communities and on our lands. During the 1992 presidential transition process, another historic step was taken as Dr. Robert Bullard[2] was chosen to represent the environmental-justice community in the environmental-transition cluster, the first time that a grass-roots movement has ever had a representative in such a process. . . .

International Developments

Perhaps the most significant evolution in the environmental-justice movement is the linkages formed with our counterparts in Third-World nations. The United Nations Conference on Environment and Development (UNCED, also known as the Earth Summit) was a catalyst for many significant developments. In March 1992, the Highlander Center, the People's Alliance, and the New York City Coalition for Environmental Justice hosted the People's Forum in New York City to

---

[2]Robert Bullard is one of the founders of the environmental justice movement. He is the director of the Environmental Justice Resource Center at Clark Atlanta University.

coincide with the fourth Preparatory Committee Meeting for UNCED, which was held at the United Nations during the entire month of March. The purpose of the People's Forum was to bring together grass-roots activists from all over the United States and their counterparts from the Third World to share our common experiences and develop strategies that could affect the negotiations at UNCED. This included a tense meeting with Ambassador William Ryan, chief U.S. representative to UNCED, regarding the participation of grass-roots activists on the official U.S. delegation to the Earth Summit. We suggested that there should be several grass-roots representatives on the U.S. delegation, and Ambassador Ryan responded that perhaps we could have one. As it turned out, there were three African American NGO observers on the official U.S. delegation at the Earth Summit, all of whom were supportive of the environmental-justice movement. At the behest of the environmental-justice movement, this was the first time that people of color outside of government were ever included as part of an official U.S. delegation to a United Nations sponsored conference. Don Edwards, then executive director of the Panos Institute USA, was designated by the environmental-justice movement as our representative on the U.S. delegation.

At the local level, another component of the effort to build the network internationally was the creation of a series of Toxic Tours, designed to take the international delegates, as well as those from other parts of the United States, into underdeveloped and environmentally degraded communities in New York City. We took bus loads of delegates to neighborhoods in Brooklyn, West Harlem, and the South Bronx. These tours enabled grass-roots activists in the United States to accomplish something that language and cultural barriers had too frequently prevented: a demonstration that poverty and underdevelopment exist even in the United States and that race, class, gender, and power are central forces of our oppression. . . .

Conclusion

As an organization that I cofounded and work with locally, West Harlem Environmental Action has grown and developed in step with the environmental-justice movement as a whole. We began as an ad hoc community coalition in 1986, and now we are a freestanding community-based organization that provides information, technical assistance and expertise, resources, and community-organizing skills to our community and to other communities like ours around New York City who are addressing the multiple environmental plagues that have beset our communities. We have greatly benefited from the wisdom of many people with whom we have been privileged to work in this movement. We have drawn strength from the trials of our brothers and sisters all over this country. What we have learned from them cannot be quantified. My comrades and I feel honored to be a part of this movement, a movement that I am certain will ultimately bring about justice for all.

A Chronology of Key Events in
U.S. Environmentalism since 1945

1945   *August 6 and 9:* The United States drops atomic bombs on the Japanese cities of Hiroshima and Nagasaki, ending World War II.

1948–
1949   William Vogt publishes *Road to Survival* and Fairfield Osborn publishes *Our Plundered Planet.* Aldo Leopold's *A Sand County Almanac* is published in 1949, a year after his death. All three books bridge the concerns between conservation and a new conception of global responsibility.

1951   The Nature Conservancy is founded. By 2000, it has 900,000 members and has protected ten million acres.

1953   Tests show radioactive iodine from testing nuclear weapons present in children in Utah.

1955   Congress passes the Air Pollution Control Act (a precursor to all subsequent clean-air legislation); smog closes schools in Los Angeles; people die from smog-related illness in New York and London throughout the decade.

1956   Congress rejects a proposal to dam part of Dinosaur National Monument at Echo Park. A dam at Glen Canyon remains part of the project.

1962   Rachel Carson publishes *Silent Spring.*

1963   Congress passes the first Clean Air Act "to improve, strengthen, and accelerate programs for the prevention and abatement of air pollution."

Portions of the chronology have been taken from William Kovarik, *Environmental History Timeline* <http://www.environmentalhistory.org>. Originally published in *Mass Media and Environmental Conflict,* Mark Neuzil and William Kovarik (Thousand Oaks, Calif.: Sage, 1996).

1964 The Wilderness Act creates a National Wilderness Preservation System with 9.1 million acres.

1965 Congress passes the Water Quality Act, the Noise Control Act, the Solid Waste Disposal Act, and the Beautification Act.

1966 Paul Ehrlich publishes *The Population Bomb.*

The Sierra Club publishes advertisements in the *New York Times* and *Washington Post* against a proposed dam that would flood the Grand Canyon.

1968 Garrett Hardin publishes "The Tragedy of the Commons" in *Science.*

1969 The Cuyahoga River in Cleveland, Ohio, catches fire from oil and chemical pollution, focusing national attention on urban water pollution.

The Santa Barbara oil spill releases more than 200,000 gallons of crude oil across thirty miles of coastline; Congress passes the National Environmental Policy Act.

1970 *April 22:* The first Earth Day.

Congress passes a series of amendments to the Clean Air Act, entirely rewriting the law. The new act sets national air quality standards, regulates emissions from motor vehicles, and allows citizens the right to sue corporations and the government for violations of emissions standards.

Natural Resources Defense Council is founded to litigate for environmental causes.

Marjory Stoneman Douglas founds Friends of the Everglades.

Environmental Protection Agency established by law.

Occupational Health and Safety Administration (OSHA) signed into law.

1972 Congress passes the Federal Water Pollution Control Act, the Coastal Zone Management Act, the Ocean Dumping Act, and the Marine Mammal Protection Act.

Donella H. Meadows and Dennis Meadows publish *Limits to Growth.*

United Nations Conference on the Human Environment convenes in Stockholm, Sweden; United Nations General Assembly establishes the UN Environmental Programme to act on the recommendations of the Stockholm meeting.

Congress bans DDT.

1973 Congress passes the Endangered Species Act.

1974 Lester Brown and others found Worldwatch Institute.

1975 Edward Abbey publishes *The Monkey Wrench Gang.*

1976 A report of the National Academy of Science warns that CFCs (chlorofluorocarbons, commonly found in refrigerators and aerosol sprays) damage the ozone layer.

1978 Lois Gibbs and her neighbors form the Love Canal Homeowners Association.

1979 The Three Mile Island nuclear power plant near Harrisburg, Pennsylvania, partially melts down, confirming environmentalists' fears about nuclear energy.

Earth First! is founded by Dave Foreman, Howie Wolke, and Mike Roselle.

James Lovelock publishes *Gaia: A New Look at Life on Earth,* theorizing that the earth is a self-regulating organism.

Global 2000, a report prepared by the Council on Environmental Quality and the Department of State on "probable changes in the world's population, natural resources and environment through the end of the century," is delivered to President Jimmy Carter.

1980 President Carter announces the relocation of 700 families in the Love Canal area of Niagara Falls, New York.

Superfund Law (CERCLA: The Comprehensive Environmental Response, Compensation and Liability Act) directs the EPA to clean up abandoned toxic waste dumps.

1984 A U.S.-owned Union Carbide Co. fertilizer plant leaks methyl ico-cyanide in Bhopal, India, killing 2,000 people. Another 8,000 die of chronic effects, and 100,000 are injured.

1985 British scientist Joe Farman publishes his discovery of an ozone hole over Antarctica, confirmed by a NASA satellite.

UN Environmental Programme begins negotiations under the Vienna Convention for the Protection of Ozone, leading to the 1987 Montreal Protocol.

1986 The Chernobyl nuclear reactor explodes in Ukraine; over 2,000 square miles are evacuated.

1987 Twenty-four countries, including the United States, sign the Montreal Protocol, an international agreement to phase out ozone-depleting chemicals.

1988 NASA scientist James Hanson warns Congress about global warming.

The World Meteorological Organization and UN Environmental Programme establish the Intergovernmental Panel on Climate Change (IPCC).

West Harlem Environmental Action is founded by Peggy Shepard, Vernice Miller, and Chuck Sutton.

1989 The oil tanker *Exxon Valdez* runs aground in Prince William Sound, Alaska, spilling 11 million gallons of oil.

1991 First National People of Color Environmental Leadership Summit, Washington, D.C.

1992 The first Earth Summit, Rio de Janeiro, Brazil.

1997 The Kyoto Protocol is adopted by 122 nations, but not ratified by the U.S. Senate; American industry predicts "disaster" if carbon dioxide reductions are enforced; environmentalists argue the treaty is too weak.

1998 The warmest year since record keeping began in 1860.

1999 The earth's population exceeds six billion.

2001 President George W. Bush's energy plan emphasizes oil exploration and new construction of coal and nuclear power plants, as well as conservation.

2003 Twelve eastern states win federal court injunctions preventing the Bush administration from weakening federal clean air laws.

2004 Kenyan environmentalist and human rights campaigner Wangari Maathai wins the Nobel Peace Prize, the first African woman to be awarded this prize, for her work in the Green Belt Movement that began in the 1970s. Maathai has planted tens of millions of trees across Africa to slow deforestation.

Questions for Consideration

1. Identify two turning points in the history of American environmentalism since 1945, and identify one document for each turning point. Explain the importance of the documents you have chosen.

2. Why is wilderness so central to the beginnings of environmentalism? What did it come to symbolize after the atomic bombs that ended World War II?

3. Environmentalists have advocated various kinds of transformation: intellectual and moral (Documents 11, 15, and 27), political (Document 20), and technological (Documents 13 and 21). Others have advocated political resistance and sabotage (Documents 19 and 22). Based on the documents presented here, what has been the ideology of environmentalism?

4. What is the environmental critique of economic growth and technological progress? Why have these concerns been so central to environmentalism? Identify three documents that critique economic growth and technological progress.

5. What is ecology and why has it been an important idea in the formation of environmentalism? In particular, what arguments are at the heart of Aldo Leopold's "Thinking like a Mountain" (Document 11) and the selection from Rachel Carson's *Silent Spring* (Document 12)? How do these authors make use of science?

6. How have women contributed to American environmentalism? Consider the work of Marjory Stoneman Douglas (Document 2), Donella Meadows (Document 9), Rachel Carson (Document 12), Lady Bird Johnson (Document 24), Lois Gibbs (Document 28), and Vernice Miller (Document 30). What is distinctive about the way women have contributed to environmentalism?

7. Where have environmentalists placed responsibility for progress toward a clean and stable environment: on industry, government, or individual consumers? Which documents speak to the role of technology in environmental improvement? Will technology solve the problems these authors see in the ways that Americans consume?

8. What is the "tragedy of the commons" (Document 7), and what does it assume about society and human behavior? Can you think of ways of resolving it, or is it inevitable?

9. What might various authors say about global warming, its causes, and how it should be confronted? Imagine responses from Rachel Carson (Document 12), Paul Ehrlich (Document 8), Barry Commoner (Document 13), and Vernice Miller (Document 30).

10. What has been the relationship between environmentalism and the U.S. government?

11. In the 1980s, various environmental organizations and philosophies appeared that many labeled "radical" environmentalism. Describe their goals and explain how they differ from the mainstream environmental movement.

Selected Bibliography

Abbey, Edward. *Desert Solitaire: A Season in the Wilderness.* New York: Ballantine Books, 1968.

Berry, Wendell. *The Unsettling of America: Culture and Agriculture.* San Francisco: Sierra Club Books, 1977.

Bullard, Robert D. *Dumping in Dixie: Race, Class, and Environmental Quality.* Boulder, Colo.: Westview Press, 1994.

Callenbach, Ernest. *Ecotopia.* Berkeley, Calif.: Banyan Tree Books, 1975.

Carson, Rachel. *Silent Spring.* New York: Houghton Mifflin, 1964.

Christofferson, Bill. *The Man from Clear Lake: Earth Day Founder Senator Gaylord Nelson.* Madison: University of Wisconsin Press, 2004.

Cohen, Michael P. *The Pathless Way: John Muir and American Wilderness.* Madison: University of Wisconsin Press, 1984.

Colten, Craig E., and Peter N. Skinner. *The Road to Love Canal: Managing Industrial Waste before EPA.* Austin: University of Texas Press, 1996.

Commoner, Barry. *The Closing Circle: Nature, Man, and Technology.* New York: Alfred A. Knopf, 1971.

Daly, Herman E. *Steady-State Economics.* San Francisco: W. H. Freeman and Company, 1977.

Devall, Bill, and George Sessions. *Deep Ecology: Living as If Nature Mattered.* Salt Lake City: G. M. Smith, 1985.

Donahue, Brian. *Reclaiming the Commons: Community Farms and Forests in a New England Town.* New Haven, Conn.: Yale University Press, 1999.

Dorman, Robert L. *A Word for Nature: Four Pioneering Environmental Advocates, 1845–1913.* Chapel Hill: University of North Carolina Press, 1998.

Douglas, Marjory Stoneman. *The Everglades: River of Grass.* New York: Rinehart, 1947.

Dowie, Mark. *Losing Ground: American Environmentalism at the Close of the Twentieth Century.* Cambridge, Mass.: MIT Press, 1996.

Ehrlich, Paul. *The Population Bomb.* New York: Ballantine Books, 1968.

Flippen, J. Brooks. *Nixon and the Environment.* Albuquerque: University of New Mexico Press, 2000.

Fox, Stephen. *The American Conservation Movement: John Muir and His Legacy*. Boston: Little, Brown, 1981.

Foreman, Dave, ed. *Ecodefense: A Field Guide to Monkeywrenching*. 1985; third edition, edited with Bill Haywood. Chico: Calif.: Abbzug Press, 1993.

Gibbs, Lois. *Love Canal: My Story*. Albany: State University of New York Press, 1983.

Gottlieb, Robert. *Forcing the Spring: The Transformation of the American Environmental Movement*. Washington, D.C.: Island Press, 1993.

Guha, Ramachandra. *Environmentalism: A Global History*. New York: Longman, 2000.

Hardin, Garrett. "The Tragedy of the Commons." *Science*. New Series 162 (December 1968): 1243–48.

Harvey, Mark W. T. *A Symbol of Wilderness: Echo Park and the American Conservation Movement*. Albuquerque: University of New Mexico Press, 1994.

Hays, Samuel P. *Beauty, Health, and Permanence: Environmental Politics in the United States, 1955–1985*. New York: Cambridge University Press, 1987.

Hays, Samuel P. *Conservation and the Gospel of Efficiency: The Progressive Conservation Movement, 1890–1920*. New York: Atheneum, 1959.

Helvarg, David. *The War against the Greens: The "Wise-Use" Movement, the New Right and Anti-Environmental Violence*. San Francisco: Sierra Club Books, 1994.

Hofrichter, Richard, ed. *Toxic Struggles: The Theory and Practice of Environmental Justice*. Philadelphia: New Society Publishers, 1993.

Intergovernmental Panel on Climate Change, Contribution of Working Group I to the Third Assessment. *Climate Change 2001: The Scientific Basis*. Cambridge: Cambridge University Press, 2001.

Kaufman, Polly Welts. *National Parks and the Woman's Voice: A History*. Albuquerque: University of New Mexico Press, 1996.

Lear, Linda J. *Rachel Carson: Witness for Nature*. New York: Henry Holt, 1997.

Leopold, Aldo. *A Sand County Almanac*. New York: Oxford University Press, 1949.

Lovins, Amory B. *Soft Energy Paths: Toward a Durable Peace*. San Francisco: Friends of the Earth, 1977.

Martinez-Alier, Joan. *The Environmentalism of the Poor: A Study of Ecological Conflicts and Calculation*. Northhampton, Mass.: Edward Elgar Publishing, 2002.

Meadows, Donella H., and Dennis Meadows. *Limits to Growth: A Report for the Club of Rome's Project on the Predicament of Mankind*. New York: Universe Books, 1972.

Muir, John. *My First Summer in the Sierra*. San Francisco: Sierra Club Books, 1988.

Oelschlaeger, Max. *The Idea of Wilderness: From Prehistory to the Age of Ecology.* New Haven, Conn.: Yale University Press, 1991.

Philippon, Daniel J. *Conserving Words: How American Nature Writers Shaped the Environmental Movement.* Athens: University of Georgia Press, 2004.

Porter, Eliot. *The Place No One Knew: Glen Canyon on the Colorado.* San Francisco: Sierra Club Books, 1963.

Rome, Adam Ward. *The Bulldozer in the Countryside: Suburban Sprawl and the Rise of American Environmentalism.* New York: Cambridge University Press, 2001.

———. "'Give Earth a Chance': The Environmental Movement and the Sixties." *Journal of American History,* 90 (September 2003): 525–54.

Rubin, Charles T. *The Green Crusade: Rethinking the Roots of Environmentalism.* New York: Free Press, 1994.

Runte, Alfred. *National Parks: The American Experience.* Lincoln: University of Nebraska Press, 1979.

Schrepfer, Susan R. *Nature's Altars: Mountains, Gender, and American Environmentalism.* Lawrence: University Press of Kansas, 2005.

Spence, Mark. *Dispossessing the Wilderness: Indian Removal and the Making of the National Parks.* New York: Oxford University Press, 1999.

Sutter, Paul S. *Driven Wild: How the Fight against Automobiles Launched the Modern Wilderness Movement.* Seattle: University of Washington Press, 2002.

Turekian, Karl L. *Global Environmental Change: Past, Present, and Future.* Upper Saddle River, N.J.: Prentice Hall, 1996.

Wilson, Edward O. *The Future of Life.* New York: Alfred A. Knopf, 2002.

World Watch. Washington, D.C.: Worldwatch Institute, 1988–.

Worster, Donald. *Nature's Economy: A History of Ecological Ideas.* New York: Cambridge University Press, 1994.

Yergin, Daniel. *The Prize: The Epic Quest for Oil, Money, and Power.* New York: Simon & Schuster, 1991.

Zakin, Susan. *Coyotes and Town Dogs: Earth First! and the Environmental Movement.* New York: Viking, 1993.

Acknowledgments (continued from p. iv)

Document 1. *Clearing Winter Storm* (1944). Photograph by Ansel Adams Collection Center for Creative Photography, University of Arizona, © Trustees of The Ansel Adams Publishing Rights Trust.

Document 2. From the book *The Everglades: River of Grass* 50th Anniversary Edition, copyright © 1997 by Marjory Stoneman Douglas. Used by permission of Pineapple Press, Inc.

Document 3. February 1954 issue of the *Sierra Club Bulletin* reprinted with permission from the Sierra Club.

Document 4. From *The Sound of Mountain Water* by Wallace Stegner. © 1969 by Wallace Stegner. Used by permission of Doubleday, a division of Random House, Inc.

Document 5. David Brower, "Foreword," in Eliot Porter, *The Place No One Knew: Glen Canyon on the Colorado* (San Francisco: Sierra Club Books, 1963), 7–9. Excerpted by permission of the Estate of David Brower.

Document 6. Reprinted by permission of Don Congdon Associates, Inc. Copyright © 1968 by Edward Abbey, renewed 1996 by Clarke Abbey.

Document 7. Reprinted with permission from Garrett Hardin, "The Tragedy of the Commons," *Science*, 162 (December 13, 1968), pp. 1243–48. Copyright © 1968 AAAS.

Document 8. From *The Population Bomb* by Dr. Paul Ehrlich, copyright © 1968, 1971 by Paul R. Ehrlich. Used by permission of Ballantine Books, a division of Random House, Inc.

Document 9. Reprinted with permission from D. H. Meadows et al., *Limits to Growth* (New York: Universe Books, 1972), 45–46, 50–54. Third Edition published as D. H. Meadows et al., *Limits to Growth — The 30-Year Update* (White River Junction, Vt.: Chelsea Green Publishing), 2004.

Document 10. From *Outgrowing the Earth: Rising Food Prices, the Growing Politics of Food Scarcity* by Lester Brown. Copyright © 2004 by Earth Policy Institute. Used by permission of W. W. Norton & Company, Inc.

Document 11. From *A Sand County Almanac and Sketches Here and There* by Aldo Leopold, copyright © 1949, 1953, 1966, renewed 1977, 1981 by Oxford University Press, Inc. Used by permission of Oxford University Press, Inc.

Document 12. "The Obligation to Endure," from *Silent Spring* by Rachel Carson. Copyright © 1962 by Rachel L. Carson, renewed 1990 by Roger Christie. Reprinted by permission of Houghton Mifflin Company. All rights reserved.

Document 13. From *The Closing Circle* by Barry Commoner, copyright © 1971 by Barry Commoner. Used by permission of Alfred A. Knopf, a division of Random House, Inc.

Document 15. Bill Devall, George Sessions excerpt from *Deep Ecology: Living as If Nature Mattered* (Salt Lake City: Peregrine Smith Books, 1985) 7–9, 67–70. Reprinted with permission from Gibbs Smith Publishers.

Document 16. Used by permission of the Intergovernmental Panel on Climate Change.

Document 17. From *The Future of Life* by Edward O. Wilson, copyright © 2002 by E. O. Wilson. Used by permission of Alfred A. Knopf, a division of Random House, Inc.

Document 19. Reprinted with permission of Denis Hayes.

Document 20. From *Ecotopia* by Ernest Callenbach, copyright © 1975 by Ernest Callenbach. Used by permission of Banyan Tree Books, a division of Random House, Inc.

Document 21. Reprinted by permission of *Foreign Affairs* (October 1976). Copyright © 1976 by the Council on Foreign Relations, Inc.

Document 22. From *Ecodefense: A Field Guide to Monkeywrenching*, copyright © 1985. Reprinted with permission of Dave Foreman and Bill Haywood.

Document 23. From *The End of Nature* by William McKibben, copyright © 1989 by William McKibben. Used by permission of Random House, Inc.

Document 25. Copyright © 1966 by Ben H. Bagdikian.

Document 27. From the *Unsettling of America: Culture and Agriculture*, by Wendell Berry. Copyright © 1977 Wendell Berry. Reprinted by permission of Sierra Club Books.

Document 28. From *Love Canal: My Story*, Lois Marie Gibbs. Reprinted by permission of Lois Marie Gibbs.

Document 29. Reprinted with permission from The César Chávez Foundation.

Document 30. Reprinted with kind permission of Vernice D. Williams.

Index

167